The Role of the Presiding Bishop

Roland Foster

Contents

Foreword: A Study of the Office

On March 30, 1981 the Right Rev. Robert C. Witcher asked me to undertake a study of the office of Presiding Bishop for the Standing Commission on Structure. In particular he asked me to look at that office in historical perspective. I agreed to accept the project; it has proved to be a fascinating one and considerably more involved than I expected at first. Virtually all of the summer and most of September have been devoted to this project.

I quickly discovered that little earlier work had been done. In 1949 the Rev. C. Rankin Barnes published a fine article on "The Presiding Bishops of the Church."[1] Ten years later William Joseph Barnds covered much the same ground in an article, "A Study of the Development of the Office of Presiding Bishop of the American Episcopal Church, 1794-1944."[2] And earlier this year, Canon Charles Guilbert gave the Johnson Lectures at Seabury-Western Theological Seminary which dealt extensively with the office of Presiding Bishop.[3] All three studies, however, concentrate on the canonical development of the office. Canons which define the various duties and responsibilities of the presiding bishop are an important part of the history of that office, but there is often a considerable gap between canonical expectations and the actual life of any part of this church. My hope was to make a much broader inquiry, to look at the actual functioning of the office and at the significant individuals who held it. I also wanted to discover the symbols and images used about the presiding bishop, which were as important — probably more important — than any canonical provisions.

Again, it was clear that there was little earlier work on which to rely. Apart from Bruce Steiner's study of Samuel Seabury, there is no standard, modern study of any of the presiding bishops. In some cases, nineteenth-century biographies exist, and in a few cases brief articles about particular presiding bishops have been published. Nor have any studies been done on the role of episcopacy in this church. This situation is a familiar one for any student of the Episcopal Church.

Fortunately, there are rich primary sources for any inquiry. The Archives of the Episcopal Church in Austin, Texas have preserved many papers, and I am indebted to Dr. Nelle Bellamy, Archivist, and to her assistant, Ms. Eleanor Hearn, for their gracious and skilled assistance in finding appropriate material. The St. Mark's Library at General Theological Seminary also has a rich collection of printed materials and has unparalleled holdings in Episcopal Church periodicals. Many of the presiding bishops have published articles, sermons, and even books; and some of their friends have published reminiscences. Bishop Sherrill's delightful autobiography, *Among Friends,* is readily available. Last year a doctoral student at General Seminary, the Rev. Charles Henery, completed a "Research Project for the Episcopal Television Network on John Elbridge Hines, Presiding Bishop"; and he has graciously allowed me to use some of his findings.

Many individuals have assisted in this project. The Right Rev. John Allin gave kind permission to use materials in the files of the presiding bishops at Austin which are less than fifty years old and therefore normally restricted. All material taken from those files has been seen and approved by the Right Rev. Milton Wood. Canon James Gundram, Bishop Wood, the Rev. Goldwaith Sherill and Mr. Robert Royce have all patiently endured and responded to my questions. Bishop Hines opened his home, his files and his heart to Fr. Henery.

Mr. F. Garner Ranney, Historiographer of the Diocese of Maryland, graciously made documents available from that rich collection. Prof. Carleton Hayden and Prof. William A. Koelsch gave me some significant citations.

My special thanks go to many students who have worked with me over the years in exploring this church's history. Their work has contributed in countless ways, recognized and unrecognized, in my own investigations. Above all, I am indebted to Bishop Witcher and the trustees of the Mercer Foundation who have commissioned and made possible this study.

None of these friends are, of course, responsible for my conclusions, and I must be held accountable for them.

Roland Foster
The General Theological Seminary
March 15, 1982

1 *Historical Magazine,* June, 1949: 97-147.

2 Ibid., Dec., 1958: 254-86.

3 Guilbert, Charles. "Changes in the Structure, Organization and Governance of the Episcopal Church in the Past Sixty Years," 1981 Johnson Lectures. These have not yet been published, and I am indebted to Bishop Witcher and Dean Edwards for advance copies of these lectures.

1: The Classic Role

The Revolutionary War was a short-term disaster not only for English interests but also for the English Church in the colonies. Most of the Anglican clergy in the middle and New England colonies were by churchmanship and temperament identified with the Society for the Propagation of the Gospel, the English cause, and the Crown. Supporters of the loyalist cause, they could expect little sympathy or support when, as one of them put it, the "spirit of disaffection and rebellion" triumphed. Further south the apparently secure establishment was withdrawn, income ceased, and more than a hundred priests and parishes found themselves without support.[1] In 1807 William White looked back on the situation in 1782 and wrote:

"[At that time] our churches were declining, almost to non-existence. In this state [Pennsylvania], there were but three clergymen . . . In the states immediately south of us, most of the clergy had ceased to officiate on the ceasing of the establishment . . . To the northward, the clergy were almost universally restrained from officiating."

Recent scholarship has considerably revised an earlier estimate that the twenty-five year period from 1785 to 1811 was one of continued organizational collapse and suspended animation. Frederick Mills has discovered that between 1785 and 1789, ninety-one new deacons were ordained; and, although records are lost, probably most became priests within a short time. Of the 314 active parishes in 1774, at least 259 and probably more were again active by 1789. In other words, at least eighty percent of prewar Anglican parishes were again functioning by the time the United States Constitution had been ratified. More recently, Charles R. Henery has studied in detail "The Episcopal Church in Post-Revolutionary

New England and New York: 1783-1811" and found a pattern of remarkable organizational recovery, especially in centers like New York, Connecticut, and Massachusetts. Henery's conclusion is worth quoting, especially for those who still think of the pre-1811 period as one of suspended animation.

"Not only had all but six of the one hundred and eight colonial parishes recovered from the rigors of the Revolution, but one hundred and forty-three new parishes were organized by 1811 ... This period witnessed the construction of one hundred new churches. One hundred and fifty-one ordinations to the diaconate were performed during these years, and whereas there had been sixty clergy in New England and New York in 1774, in 1811 there numbered ninety-seven clergy. And the establishment of diocesan institutions and societies, as well as the publications of literary works, testified to a Church more than willing to provide itself with the energy and materials necessary for its nurture and training."[2]

The major question which Anglicans faced after the Treaty of Paris was not simply the matter of organizational recovery and a new administrative structure but the deeper question of identity and self-understanding. Such questions can also be important for an established church, but an established church gains much of its identity merely by being established. The Church of England can be understood in part as the established church to which, until a century or less ago, all English men and women belonged, at least in theory, except for a few dissenters. But a voluntarist denomination faces more serious problems and is under much greater pressure to articulate its identity. All of the great emerging national denominations instinctively understood that need, and those which grew soon developed rituals and symbolic ways of expressing their identity with great power.

Anglicanism probably faced a greater problem of redefining its identity than any other major American religious tradition. Indeed the major achievement of the post-Revolutionary period was not that of erecting a new canonical and legislative structure but the more difficult task of articulating a new ecclesiological and symbolic understanding of an American Anglicanism. The preface to the Prayer Book of 1789 put the problem quite concisely:

"When in the course of Divine Providence, these American States became independent with respect to civil government, their ecclesiastical independence was necessarily included; and the different religious denominations of Christians in these States were left at full and equal liberty to model and organize their respective Churches, and forms of worship, and discipline, in such manner as they might judge most convenient for their future prosperity; *consistently with the constitution and the laws of their country.*" (Emphasis added.)

That preface might go on to affirm that "this Church is far from intending to depart from the Church of England in any essential point of doctrine, discipline, or worship; or further than local circumstances require," but as far as both government and identity were concerned, local circumstances required quite a bit!

The preface puts the question almost entirely in canonical and legislative terms, but the actual question of identity had deeper ramifications. The Second Great Awakening was sweeping the country. Revivalism, extemporaneous prayer, conversion, pietism were marks of a new and expanding protestantism. Since the 1740s, Anglicanism has been known for its virtually unanimous opposition to revivals, and the Second Awakening found little response among Episcopalians. Thus American Anglicans not only faced the problem of defining their identity in respect to the Church of England but of defining and commending that identity in the face of an aggressive Congregationalism and Presbyterianism and an emerging and powerful Baptist and Methodist revivalist tradition.

The development of a new canonical structure has often been told, but the emergence of a new symbolic identity has been less fully explored by historians. Bishop William White was one of the first to define it in terms of the Thirty-Nine Articles, the Prayer Book, and the three-fold ministry of bishops, priests, and deacons. White never deviated from that understanding. As late as 1826 he defined the "enumerated particulars" of the American church as "the doctrines of grace as contained in our articles . . . the worshipping of God in a prescribed form of prayer . . . and the three orders of the ministry instituted by the Apostles."[3] By 1826, however, that understanding had already been considerably deepened by men like John Henry Hobart. The problem with White's definition was that it failed to carry much power or conviction to a voluntarist American people. Sydney Mead and others have pointed out that an appeal to church history was for the most part irrelevant for American Protestantism. There was simply no common history to appeal to. Holy Scripture remained the sole basis for authority.[4] It was the genius of Hobart to see that Articles, prayer book, and episcopacy must be put within the context of scriptural authority if they were to commend themselves to future members. He did so not by debating particular New Testament texts but simply by arguing that the early church was a church marked above by liturgy, apostolic ministry, and the evangelical truth of justification by faith alone enshrined in the Articles. "Evangelical truth and apostolic order" became Hobart's watchword and challenge.

Here are two typical quotations from Hobart which assert the authority of the early church and which see episcopacy within that authoritative structure.

"Is High Churchman then, brethren, an appellation of which we should be ashamed? No! Let it be our boast, unpopular as it can be, only as it is misunderstood. The principles which it covers, are those of the first and purest ages of Christianity, of the age of the apostles, of martyrs and confessors.

"[This church adheres] in all essential points to the faith, ministry and worship which distinguished the apostolic and primitive Church, and particularly to the constitution of the Christian ministry under its three orders of Bishops, Priests and Deacons."

Episcopacy, in other words, was an "essential point" of the church's order, and Hobart had no hesitation in declaring nonepiscopal ministries invalid.

"I could not maintain the divine authority of the Episcopal ministry without denying the validity of a non-episcopal ministry; for it is an essential principle in the episcopal ministry that Bishops, as an order superior to Presbyters, have alone the power of ordination. Of course a ministry not episcopally ordained, cannot be a valid ministry."[5]

It is little wonder that a prominent New York Presbyterian characterized Hobart's views as "of such deep-toned horror, as may well make one's hair to stand up like quills upon the fretful porcupine, and freeze the warm blood at the fountain."[6]

When we look at the relatively modest roles of bishops and the presiding bishop during this classic period, it is important to remember that the seeds of a far richer and more expanded understanding of those offices were powerfully set forth in the earliest days of this church's national history.

One important corrolary of the appeal to the early Church was an emphasis placed upon stability, conservatism, and hostility to change. An unchanging prayer book was held up as a sign of a church which remained steadfast in its loyalty to the early Church; and it was not until 1892, when this classic vision of Episcopal identity was undergoing remarkable transformation, that prayer book revision was possible. The image of the rock began to emerge as a symbol of this church. In one of the more interesting juggling of New Testament images, Bishop William Whittingham explained to the Presbyterians of South Orange in 1829 that Christ is "the Rock, and the Way, and the Life" and defended liturgy and episcopacy as the way of the early Church.[7] Henry Clay is attributed (perhaps incorrectly) with a statement confirming the conservative character of the Episcopal Church.

"Years of observation and study have led me to the conclusion that the stability of our government depends upon the perpetuation of two institutions. One of these and the more important of the two is the Episcopal Church and the other is the Supreme Court of the United States."[8]

A more typical expression of this sense of stability was Horatio Potter's sermon in 1843 on "The Stability of the Church."

"Whoever will examine either the history of our Church, or the principles on which it is founded, will be constrained to admit that it is *not given to change* . . . Such as it was established in this country, soon after the American revolution, such has it remained ever since, without the slightest alteration in its principles or in its practices, in its doctrines, or in its discipline and worship; and that, too, with a degree of internal harmony and peace, which is without a parallel in any other denomination in this country."[9]

For the purposes of this account, it is probably unnecessary to expand on this emerging identity any further; but it is very important to see the developing offices of bishop and presiding bishop against this theological and ecclesiological background and not merely as a matter of canonical legislation.

As far as I know, there is no serious study of the actual role of episcopacy in the early Episcopal Church, and this next section is tentatively offered as a first exploration into largely uncharted waters.

When Samuel Seabury was consecrated in Aberdeen, Scotland in 1784 he signed a concordat with the Scottish bishops. Article Two affirmed not only the civil independence of the new church but also the ecclesial independence of the episcopate.

> "Under Him [Christ] the chief ministers or managers of the affairs of this spiritual society are those called Bishops, whose exercise of their sacred office being independent of all lay powers, it follows, of consequence, that their spiritual authority and jurisdiction cannot be affected by any lay deprivation."[10]

Bishop Skinner of Scotland probably had in mind the deprivation of 1689; but in America, this provision meant Seabury's insistence on a separate House of Bishops, canonical equality with the House of Deputies, and assurance that bishops would be tried only by episcopal courts. In fact, Seabury won almost all of his points. Although the 1789 Constitution provided that the House of Bishops could be overridden by a four-fifths vote of the House of Deputies, a separate House was assured and bishops would be tried only by bishops.

Impressive as were these achievements in maintaining continuity with the Church of England, the contrasts should also be noted. The late Eighteenth Century Church of England had neither diocesan, metropolitan, nor national synods apart from Parliament itself; and its ranks of ministry were far more elaborate than the simple one of bishop, presbyters, and deacons. Archbishops, bishops, deans, archdeacons, prebends, canons, rectors, vicars, etc., marked the complex and sometimes contradictory structure of the Church of England. By contrast, the working American structure of bishops, ministers and church wardens was a far simpler and more logical one.[11] As early as 1785 the General Convention, in considering an appeal to the English bishops and archbishops, noted that the more elaborate titles and structure of the English bench would not be appropriate here.

"Whereas the Bishops of this Church will not be entitled to any of such temporal honors as are due to the Archbishops and Bishops of the parent Church . . . and whereas the reputation and usefulness of our Bishops will considerably depend on their taking no higher titles or stile than will be due to their spiritual employments; that it be recommended to this Church . . . to provide that their respective Bishop may be called "The Right Rev. A. B. Bishop of the Protestant Episcopal Church in C.D.," and, as a Bishop, may have no other title."[12]

Although histories of well-known early Episcopal Bishops usually concentrate on their episcopal activities, it seems clear that most of them spent most of their time as parish ministers. William White was rector of Christ Church, St. Peter's and St. James', Philadelphia; John Henry Hobart was rector of Trinity Church, St. Paul's, and St. John's Chapel, New York, as were the two previous bishops of New York; Alexander Griswold was consecrated bishop of the Eastern Diocese in 1811 but remained rector of St. Peter's Church, Salem, Massachusetts; John Croes was not only bishop of the Church in New Jersey but also rector of Christ Church, New Brunswick. The Canons of 1795 required bishops to visit every parish in their jurisdiction once in three years and added that, ". . . it shall be the duty of the clergy, in such reasonable rotation as may be devised, to officiate for him in any parochial duties which belong to him,"[13] but the canon was difficult to implement. In 1811 Bishop White reported to the Convention of Pennsylvania that, ". . . my constant course of parochial duty has prevented me from visiting any neighbouring Church" and added that "the number of persons confirmed by me, all in the city [of Philadelphia] has been sixty-one."[14] Hobart went on justly-famous visitation tours, but a careful study of their dates shows that they often were limited to one or two months. In 1820, for example, he spent much of July and August visiting churches, sometimes at the rate of three a week; but he was in New York for the rest of the year.[15] In 1822 John Croes of New Jersey visited eleven parishes.[16] One of the more conscientious visitors was Alexander Griswold who reported to his Convention in 1828:

"The rule, which from the first I have adopted, is, that every Church, however remote, shall be visited once in two years; and more than two-thirds have I been able to visit *every* year. Were I released from the care of a parish, or if my pecuniary resources would admit of my employing an assistant in it, my duty certainly would be to go through the whole Diocese every year."[17]

In 1835 Griswold was released from parochial duties and was exclusively involved in diocesan responsibilities until his death in 1843.

It seems safe to assume that none of the early founders of the Episcopal Church entertained any idea of a primate, metropolitan, archbishop, or presiding bishop. There is no mention of a presiding officer in the constitution or canons of 1789, although Seabury's principle that "the bishops of this church, when there shall be three or more, shall, whenever General Conventions are held, form a separate House,"[18] was adopted in the Constitution of October, 1789. The first rule of order of the House declared that "the senior Bishop present shall be the President"[19] and Bishop Seabury took the chair. The next General Convention of 1792 modified the rule and decreed instead that "the office of President of this house shall be held in rotation, beginning from the north"[20] and Bishop Provoost presided. The first known reference to the term "Presiding Bishop" is in the rubric

14

before the service for the Consecration of a Bishop added to the Prayer Book in 1792, and three years later Bishop White signed the minutes of the Convention of that year as the "Presiding Bishop."[21] Although Bishop White presided at all of the Conventions from 1795 until his death, the rule of order of the house providing that "the senior Bishop present at the opening of any Convention, shall preside"[22] was not restored until 1804. In 1799 the canons used the phrase "presiding Bishop" for the first time: "The right of calling special meetings of the General Convention, shall be in the Bishops; this right shall be exercised by the presiding Bishop."[23]

Thus the office of Presiding Bishop appears to have begun simply as an administrative convenience. Someone was needed to preside at meetings of the House of Bishops (or prior to the formation of two houses, in October, 1789, at the unicameral General Convention); and the senior bishop present was a natural choice, especially when that senior bishop was as judicious and moderate a person as William White.

With Seabury's death in 1796, White was not only the senior bishop but also the outstanding living person who had helped in the reformation of the church during the difficult 1784-1789 years. The first clear sign of his activity as presiding bishop outside the meetings of the House of Bishops was as presiding consecrator at the consecration of bishops. Prior to 1820 the canons allowed newly-elected bishops to forward their testimonials "to any three Bishops of this church" but in fact William White's name appears without exception as the chief consecrator at every consecration from that of Robert Smith in 1795 to Jackson Kemper in 1835, a year before his death. In 1820 the canons put into law what had long been the practice of expecting the presiding bishop to take order for all episcopal consecrations.

To take order for consecrations and to preside at many consecrations may be more significant than appears at first. The symbolic and quasi-sacramental character of the office of presiding bishop is one of the more striking characteristics of that office as it developed in the Nineteenth Century; nowhere is that symbolic character seen more clearly than at the consecrations of bishops. William White presided at twenty-six consecrations. His successor, Alexander Viets Griswold, might complain that he was too old and ill to be presiding bishop, but in fact he presided at six of the ten consecrations during his term. And Philander Chase was the presiding consecrator at every episcopal consecration during the first four years of his term as presiding bishop (from 1844 until 1847) when ill health made further participation impossible. A careful study of the table of Succession of American Bishops shows an unbroken pattern. Beyond presiding at meetings of the House of Bishops, the most ancient and widespread duty of the presiding bishop has been as chief consecrator at the consecration of bishops of this church. Just as bishops first gained prominence and recognition in this church through their liturgical functions of ordaining and confirming, so the presiding bishop made his first churchwide impact as the principle consecrator and presiding liturgical officer at the most significant diocesan service, the consecration of a new bishop.

The most important new responsibility of the presiding bishop developed only during the final years of William White's term. Growing concern for the establishment of a national missionary society led to the adoption of a constitution for a voluntary Episcopal Missionary Society by the Convention of 1820. That constitution provided that "the presiding bishop *of this church* shall be the president of this society."[24] The constitution had to be hastily revised at a special convention the next year when it was discovered that bishops had been inadvertently forbidden to participate in its government, but the presiding bishop *of the church* was again made the president.[25] Significantly, the first time the presiding bishop is described as "of this church" rather than of the House of Bishops was in connection with his responsibilities for the mission of the church.

In 1822 White issued a stirring appeal for support of the new Missionary Society:

"While the active members of our church have been occupied in repairing the decayed ways and renewing the dilapidated buildings of our Zion, new prospects have been opening on them westward . . . The time is come [to supply] . . . the spiritual wants of those who have migrated from our soil, as our forefathers migrated from the land of their nativity."

He also noted that there were additional prospects of foreign missions, for ". . . the good providence of God is opening new prospects of the bringing of heathen people within the pale of the church of Christ."[26]

White brought to the office of Presiding Bishop a sense of moderation and judicious balance that characterized his entire ministry. Shortly after White's death, the Bishop of New Jersey, George Washington Doane, spoke of the style and influence of the late presiding bishop:

"In the revision of the Prayer Book as in all of the measures of that day, he was most active and influential . . . In every transaction of her councils, his wisdom has been prominent, and his agency conspicuous . . . He has been first in everything, and everything has been identified with him . . . He was regarded, with unanimus reverence and love, not for his years so much as for his mild paternal rule, the PATRIARCH of our household of faith."[27]

Professor Bird Wilson of General Seminary made the same point when writing of White in 1839. His duties ". . . were performed with so much judgment, prudence and integrity as to avoid the excitement of jealousy or dissatisfaction on account of his increased power and influence."[28]

His increased power and influence were considerable.

17

In 1804 he prepared, at the request of the House of Deputies, a syllabus of theological education which was approved by the House of Bishops that year and which remained for many years the official standard of theological education in the church. Again, he was the author of every pastoral letter issued by the House of Bishops during his lifetime. His counsel was sought in a variety of ecclesiastical concerns. For example, in 1811 the church in Virginia had been unable to secure a quorum for a diocesan (or state) convention. On June 6th, Bishop White wrote Bishop James Madison of Virginia recommending a moderate and sensible solution:

"The situation of the church in Virginia is a subject of great grief . . . You have in vain endeavoured to gather a Convention for several years. Will you permit a brother bishop to suggest a remedy . . . Your incorporation required forty to make a quorum. And although the act has been repealed, I suppose you adhere to the number. Would it not be best to consider the Constitution defunct and to form anew a convention consisting of those clergymen and deputies however far, who have zeal enough to step forward to keep the church from sinking. I am the more free to suggest this, as I believe it to be the very measure which the General Convention would set on foot if there were no bishop in Virginia."[29]

By the time of White's death in 1836 the office of presiding bishop had become much more than a canonical convenience limited to the matter of presiding at the House of Bishops. The presiding bishop had become the chief liturgical figure in the church as well as the president of its young and struggling national Missionary Society. His counsel was weighty and his opinion sought. Much of this influence can be attributed to the character and ministry of the man himself. In less judicious hands, the increasing authority of the office would arouse hestiation and even resentment.

In 1836, at the age of seventy, Alexander Viets Griswold found that he had become the presiding bishop. Bishop Onderdonk of New York at once wrote him urging him to attend a meeting of the Missionary Society. Griswold's reply was something less than enthusiastic, and significantly he began the long and ongoing debate about the nature of the office:

"I doubt the wisdom of making the oldest of our body the presiding Bishop. It is true, that his peculiar duties are not many, but they are something; and by this rule they will frequently, as in the present instance, fall upon one, who resides far from the center . . . I would prefer that he should be the Bishop of New York, or of Philadelphia. And, (as in the present case also,) those duties will often, if not always fall upon one, who, by reason of old age, is least capable of performing them . . . But we must take things as they are."

And he made plans to make a trip to New York. However, he did not want to continue the tradition of writing pastoral letters for the House of Bishops.

"A Pastoral Letter is to be prepared. For many years this has been done by one [Bishop White] in whom we all confided, but whose face we shall see no more. This surely, will not henceforth be considered as the duty, *ex officio,* of the Senior Bishop. For several good reasons, I should decline it."[30]

However, in fact, he did write the two pastoral letters that were issued during his term as presiding bishop. And in 1841 a canon "On the Trial of Bishops" provided that a presentment for a trial would be addressed to the presiding bishop, thus further deepening the tie between the presiding bishop and the episcopate of the church.[31]

Like White, Bishop Griswold exercised his authority with moderation, restraint, and even reluctance. Such was not the style of his successor, Philander Chase, the irrepressible Bishop of Illinois, who became presiding bishop in 1843 at the age of sixty-seven. Some of his actions quickly aroused the ire of his fellow bishops, especially in the east.

There were many signs of conflict. Following a long tradition, Bishop Chase wrote the pastoral letter of 1844. It consisted largely of an open attack on the Tractarians at a time when conflict was high: "How widely spread among the Romanists is the opinion that the sacrifices of the Christian altar atone for sin! Yes, not only in the Roman Church, but in some who pretend to have rejected her errors, the same dreadful perversion of the truth seems to prevail." And in a thinly veiled reference to the ordination of Arthur Carey (a New York candidate who had been charged with holding "sentiments . . . in too close conformity with the Church at Rome"), Chase threatened, "We feel it is our duty to declare that no person should be ordained who is not well acquainted with the landmarks which separate us from the Church of Rome."[32]

A very different hand wrote the next pastoral letter with its announced resolution not ". . . to repeat warnings of the past but to turn to topics of a more practical nature . . . about which, surely, there can be no diversity of sentiment whatever."[33] And the House of Deputies of the same convention rebuked Chase by refusing to confirm the election of the Rev. James B. Britton as an assistant bishop of Illinois and virtually accused Chase of manipulating the canon which allowed an assistant bishop to be elected only when the bishop is old and permanently infirm.[34]

In 1850 the House of Bishops took the unusual step of refusing to issue any pastoral letter and instead asked the presiding bishop to honor them with an address.[35] Chase returned to his favorite theme of the dangers of Romanism, which led one correspondent to the *Protestant Churchman* to regret the absence of a pastoral letter:

"The testimony of the closing address from the venerable presiding Bishop was clear and strong in condemnation of the Romanising tendencies among us. But even that could not secure the sanction of the House of Bishops. It was not put forth as a pastoral. It comes before the Church as the individual counsel of one of her Bishops, and no more."[36]

But the House was not about to accept the same kind of letter from Chase which it had approved six years earlier. In fact, the Bishop of Western New York, William H. Delancey, moved a resolution which would have, in effect, removed Chase as presiding bishop.

"Resolved, That the term of office of the Presiding Bishop be henceforth limited to three years, and that the Bishop now next in succession hold the office from and after the close of this General Convention, for three years, to the close of the next Triennial General Convention."[37]

The high point of dissatisfaction with the presiding bishop was probably reached the following year. On March 12, the London *Guardian* published a letter "to the Archbishop and Bishops and other Authorities of the Church of England and Ireland" which was signed, "Philander Chase, the Presiding Bishop of the Protestant Episcopal Church in the United States." In his letter, Chase warmly commended the established character of the Church of England and thanked God that ". . . you are protected by a civil power; . . . may that union between you and such a Christian Government continue unimpaired." William Whittingham, Bishop of Maryland, was furious. He sent a private (and later a public) protest to many bishops in this church and received virtually unanimous support from them. In his Declaration,

Whittingham wrote that ". . . the Senior Bishop of this Church neither has nor acquires by his seniority among the bishops . . . any right of corresponding with the ecclesiastical authorities of other Churches in the name of this Church, or as the representative of its bishops, or with any claim of rank, authority, or official character." Nor did Whittingham's support come only from eastern bishops. One of the strongest letters arrived from Jackson Kemper, then Bishop of Wisconsin. Kemper acknowledged receipt of the Declaration and Protest and added:

"In that declaration and protest I cordially agree; and I heartily thank you for the manly and Christian stand you have taken in reference to the conduct of a Bishop who by his bold and unauthorized exertions, his strange behaviour, his ungovernable temper and his unforgiving disposition had often injured the Church and disgraced a station which was held for many years by the meek, gentlemanly, and pure minded White.

If Bishop Meade and his friends will not present him for trial, why cannot every honourable Bishop write in making known to the Bishop of Illinois his actual position and the many causes of complaint which exist against him? I am ready to do so."[38]

It was clear that the present presiding bishop was no longer "meek" and "gentlemanly!" Some historians have little sympathy with Chase's provocative actions. Richard Solomon, who wrote extensively on the history of this church, argued that ". . . the ten years from 1843 to 1853 . . . are the most unpleasant chapter in the history of the Church . . . A good deal of the responsibility for the distressing status of those years falls on the hot-tempered man whom the rule of seniority had put into the office of Presiding Bishop.."[39]

Perhaps. But other interpretations are possible. White and Griswold had embodied an ideal of the presiding bishop as moderate, fair, impartial, presiding above conflict and dissent. That was a powerful idea; and, as we will see, it was an ideal frequently invoked in praise of later presiding bishops. Chase lived in stormier times and on a rougher, more confrontational frontier. As priest, bishop of two jurisdictions, founder of two colleges, and finally as presiding bishop, he proclaimed the truth of the gospel as he understood the same. Fear and detestation of the Church of Rome was one of his deepest convictions. In Philander Chase we see clearly for the first time a presiding bishop who sees his duty to "speak God's words to the Church and to the world."[40] His vision was a more controversial and provocative one than his predecessors held, but it has remained as a continuing tradition in this church's understanding of the presiding bishop. Indeed, one of the major tensions about the office has been that between the presiding bishop as impartial, presiding representative and the presiding bishop as spokesman —often controversial spokesman — of the gospel as he comprehends that gospel.

Bishop Chase died in 1851 following an accident, and there must have been considerable relief in many episcopal homes when the rule of seniority designated Thomas Church Brownell as presiding bishop. Brownell had been the bishop of Connecticut since 1819. In 1851 he was seventy-two and his active ministry was largely over. During his episcopate he had founded Trinity College and sixty-five parishes as well as assisting in the founding of the Diocese of Louisiana, Mississippi, and Alabama. By 1845 his health was failing and he requested the Diocese of Connecticut to elect an assistant, which they did in 1851. Understandably, he was able to do little as presiding bishop. He presided over only six of the twenty-five consecrations which took place during his term. He attended the General Conventions of 1853 and 1856 but "by reason of his advanced years, and the distance of the place of meeting from his residence" did not attend the Conventions of 1859 or 1863.[41] When he died on January

11, 1865 at the age of eighty-five, he was the senior bishop of the Anglican Communion!

Yet the years from 1853 to 1865 were momentous ones for this church. The Muhlenberg Memorial of 1853 was the most important and farsighted proposal of its day, foreshadowing many major developments yet to come. It is significant that the Memorial, and the Memorial Papers (or questionnaires) which followed, ignored completely the question of canonical and structural reform. Liturgical worship, theological education, a deeper and more comprehensive understanding of the nature of the church and its call to unity were at the forefront of the memorialists' interests. Those who were most concerned about the renewal of the church in the mid-Nineteenth Century did not see questions of church structure as central to their concern.

These years also saw this nation hurtling toward a civil war which was, on almost every count, our most traumatic and disastrous war. One consequence of that conflict was the temporary division of the Episcopal Church into two, although for some time in the early 1860s that division looked far from temporary. In all of these matters Brownell was silent. Indeed in 1856, nine years before his death, he had told the Convention of Connecticut that ". . . old age, and bodily infirmities have disqualified me for the performance of active labors; and a sense of decaying mental powers renders me diffident, even in giving counsel."[42]

No previous presiding bishop had been as inactive as Brownell necessarily was during his twelve-year term of office, and his inactivity prompted some speculation about some alternatives. In 1853 Bishop DeLancey renewed his proposal of 1850 which would limit the term to three years, although possibly in deference to the presence of Brownell, he added a new proviso that "the present presiding Bishop hold the office for three years from and after the close of this General Convention."

Bishop Alonzo Potter of Pennsylvania moved a substitute which actually passed in 1853 only to be rejected three years later. Potter's proposal was less sweeping although it did not provide for a rotating presidency of the House of Bishops.

"The Senior Bishop of this Church is the Presiding Bishop for all purposes mentioned in the Constitution and Canons.

"The Senior Bishop of this Church, present at any Consecration of a Bishop, is the Presiding Bishop for that solemnity.

"The duty of presiding over the deliberations of the Bishops assembled as a part of the General Convention, or otherwise, shall devolve on the Bishops in rotation, for the term of three years each, beginning with the Senior Bishop."[43]

Potter's proposal would have, in effect, fragmented the office with different persons fulfilling parts of the office at different times. Both proposals were recognitions that an inactive presiding bishop created problems, since inevitably the canonical duties had steadily increased as the church grew. In 1856 the canon on "The Trial of a Bishop" charged the presiding bishop to choose a board of inquiry of sixteen persons to investigate the charges. Three years later the Episcopal congregation in Paris requested and were placed under the superintendence of the presiding bishop. For the first time, the presiding bishop exercised jurisdiction over a congregation and over clergymen outside the bounds of his own diocese.[44] The General Convention itself was becoming a larger, more unwieldy body requiring more from a presiding officer. In 1820 the Convention met in Philadelphia for nine days. Eight bishops, thirty-six clerical and twenty-seven lay deputies attended. In 1858 the Convention met in Richmond, Virginia for eighteen days. Thirty-six bishops, 131 clerical and 106 lay deputies attended. General Convention had grown from seventy-one to 273 members in less than forty years.

Furthermore, in 1865 the church faced one of its major structural tests — would it reunite or would it continue as two churches, one northern and the other southern. Many of the other great national denominations had divided; that division remained permanent for the Methodists, the Baptists, and the Presbyterians. The future was by no means clear in 1865, and the usual interpretation that the Episcopal Church avoided permanent schism simply by noninvolvement in political matters has been seriously questioned by recent scholarship.

When Bishop Brownell died on January 13, 1865 the surviving senior bishop was one of the most colorful figures of the Nineteenth-Century church, John Henry Hopkins, Bishop of Vermont. It would have been hard to have chosen a more suitable person as presiding bishop during the difficult post-Civil War days. He was then seventy-three and had been Bishop of Vermont since 1832. His son and biographer reports that the new presiding bishop renewed a complaint made years earlier by another New England bishop, Alexander Griswold:

"What could be more absurd, he would often say to me, than to make the Bishop of such an out-of-the-way, little, insignificant Diocese of Vermont the Presiding Bishop of so vast a National Church as ours. The office, he thought, according to the almost universal practice and law of the Primitive Church, should belong as a matter of course to the Bishop of New York or Philadelphia."[45]

But Hopkins had no intention of remaining inactive. Indeed a memorial address after his death noted that his three years as presiding bishop ". . . added largely to his ordinary cares and labors. No one who has yet occupied the office of Presiding Bishop has been called on to undertake so many and such extended journeys or found his position beset with so many calls that involved active duty."[46]

Hopkins' sympathies with the south were well-known. Some of his closest friends were southern bishops. A year before the war began, Hopkins joined Bishops Leonidas Polk of Louisiana and Stephen Elliott of Georgia at Sewanee to lay out the proposed campus of the University of the South. Hopkins' son described the meeting:

"The few days spent in the congenial society of those two remarkable men, were highly enjoyed by my Father: and I have often heard him refer to them in a way which proved the loving warmth with which they had impressed his memory. After full conference and exchange of views concerning the great work, they left the mountain two days after Christmas. . . . He never saw either of them again, on earth."[47]

Hopkins also followed the tradition of many centuries in arguing that slavery was condoned by the Bible, and in 1861 he published a full defense of southern slavery entitled a *Bible View of Slavery*. The work was reprinted in 1863 amid considerable protest in the north. Probably no northern bishop was able to commend the cause of reunion of the church more effectively to southern white Episcopalians than was John Henry Hopkins.

Tensions were high in 1865. Three years earlier the House of Bishops had issued a pastoral letter, over Hopkins' protest, which condemned the "dark tide" of rebellion and declared that those who resist "the Constitution and government of the United States . . . shall receive to themselves damnation."[48] Bishop McIllvaine of Ohio was the author. On May 6, 1865 the *Episcopal Recorder* of Philadelphia called for striking reprisals. Men like Bishops Elliott and Wilmer ". . . have thrown themselves into the hot and senseless and causeless passions of the hour and declaimed with passionate vehemence against the North." They were both rebels and felons and "should not be the last to suffer the penalties of treason." Two weeks later the *Recorder* returned to the same theme. We have just seen, the editor wrote, "a dingy little sheet called the Southern Churchman" in which a bishop reflected with great sorrow on the meaning of defeat. The *Recorder* commented:

"In our judgment, a more simple document, confessing the sins of slavery and rebellion . . . would have been more to the purpose."[49]

Hopkins was determined to take the initiative in inviting the southern leaders back and to do everything possible to avoid any act of judgment which might alienate them. On June 22, 1865 he sent the draft of a circular letter to the northern bishops asking them to join with him in an invitation to the southern church. All refused to sign; even the most sympathetic argued that southern bishops must take the initial step. Accordingly, Hopkins sent a letter on July 12th to the southern bishops, over his own signature, ". . . as the Senior Bishop . . . to assure you personally of the cordial welcome which awaits you at our approaching General Convention;" and he added that he was certain the other bishops "sympathize with me generally in the desire to see the fullest representation of churches from the South, and to greet their brethren in the Episcopate with the kindest feelings."

Only two bishops did come to Philadelphia that October, Atkinson of North Carolina and Lay of Arkansas. The account of the reunion of Atkinson and Hopkins is justly one of the most famous in this church. Hopkins' son reported that as he was entering St. Luke's Church, Philadelphia,

"I saw, leaning against the iron railing at the halfway landing, the beloved Bishop Atkinson, of North Carolina, and round him a group of clergy and laity, welcoming him most cordially. He was the first Southern Bishop I had seen since the War began: and while joining my congratulations to those of the others, my Father came up the steps, and I had the delight of witnessing the greeting between the two, when both their hearts seemed too full to permit of easy utterance.

"All united — none more strongly than my Father — in urging the Bishop of North Carolina to return at once to his own place, and enter, robed, in the procession with his brethren. But he steadily refused: giving as his reason, his delicate regard for his Southern brethren who had not come on. . . . But when, in the midst of the service, the call was again made upon him, openly and by name, he could refuse no longer, but rose, advanced, and was welcomed at the Altar with joyful thanksgiving."[50]

And in the course of the convention, Hopkins successfully managed to prevent that body from passing any resolution of condemnation of the South or even of congratulation for the northern victory. The *Episcopal Recorder* was furious and noted with dismay that the convention ". . . refused to return thanks for the restoration of the Union and the destruction of slavery . . . This was the universal feeling of the Convention. Nothing could exceed the kindness, cordiality and fraternal affection with which the return of our Southern brethren was welcomed."[51]

No doubt different judgments will be passed on Hopkins' actions. He showed little understanding of the horrors of slavery or of the price that unionists had paid to maintain the national union. But his actions were probably decisive in bringing about the reunion of the Episcopal Church. One might speculate on a different scenario if Hopkins had not been alive in 1865. The next senior bishops were Bosworth Smith of Kentucky (who actually succeeded Hopkins in 1868) and the archunionist, Charles McIlvaine of Ohio. It seems reasonable to assume that the story of the reunion of the Episcopal Church would have been very different if Hopkins had not been presiding bishop.[52] At no previous time in the history of this church had a presiding bishop acted more decisively and effectively during a period of crisis. Hopkins was not, of course, solely responsible for the reunion of the church; but his actions were of enormous and perhaps decisive importance. He demonstrated, as had no previous presiding bishop, the enormous potential for leadership and action which the office might embody.

Beneath Hopkins's actions was a view of the office which entailed a sense of responsibility for the whole church. His role at the General Convention of 1865 was the most dramatic expression of that conception of that office, but in his address to the Convention of Vermont in 1866 he underscored that same sense of churchwide responsibility even in the more mundane matters of consecrations and administration. "I had the privilege," he reported, "of consecrating, as the Presiding Bishop, with the aid of my colleagues, the Rev. Dr. Quintard for the Diocese of Tennessee." He mentioned other consecrations and noted that he "was specially invited, as the Presiding Bishop, to attend the first of the appointed Delegate Meetings of the Board of Missions." And then he concluded by reflecting on the meaning of these actions:

"I place these extraneous facts before you, my beloved brethren, on the present occasion, although they do not directly belong to my regular duties as the Bishop of Vermont. For I doubt not that you will share my interest in them, not only because the Church of our Lord is one . . . but specially because my office as the *Presiding Bishop* connects me, of necessity, with the whole in a practical sense, which only attaches to this position; and brings you, through your Bishop, into an intimate relation with other dioceses, which did not previously exist, and perhaps may never exist again."[51]

Hopkins' vision of his role as presiding bishop was not a new one; William White had much the same. In fact, a sound interpretation of Hopkins will see him primarily as a conservative. Henry Codman Potter made a most astute observation when he wrote that Hopkins "was the first bishop of his day who ventured to wear a beard" and for that reason "though ecclesiastically conservative, was regarded as offensively eccentric."[54] Hopkins's view of slavery as biblically authorized, his determination to avoid any church involvement in politics, his overriding concern for the unity and stability of the church all place him squarely within the early Nineteenth Century understanding of Episcopal identity. His views on the role of the presiding bishop are part of that cloth. The presiding bishop stood above conflict, concerned for all parties but even more concerned for the welfare, stability, and prosperity of the entire church. He was the one person who was symbolically a figure for the whole church and who could, in moments of crisis, act decisively to appeal to and to restore that unity and stability.

With the exception of Philander Chase, all of the presiding bishops discussed in this section subscribed to and embodied that classic ideal. The presiding bishop was chiefly seen in the eyes of the church as the principal minister at episcopal consecrations. In the House of Bishops he was expected to preside impartially, to appoint committees with an even hand, and to enable "Zion" to maintain her rock-like stability. Although the Constitution of the Domestic and Foreign Missionary Society made him *ex officio* president as early as 1820, there is little evidence in the records that he was actively involved in the ordinary administration of that body. Rarely did he even attend the annual meetings. His duties for the most part lay in his diocese (and during the early part of the century, in his parish). If he had the health and the character, he could at times exercise considerable influence; but his office was primarily liturgical and ecclesiastical, not administrative. Presiding bishops might complain about being too old; their complaints were part of a general chorus from many aged diocesan bishops who were all forbidden to retire under the canons. But as long as the presiding bishop was seen primarily as a liturgical and ecclesiastical person, old age and infirmity were serious but not fatal handicaps. Only when a new understanding of this church's identity and mission developed, an understanding which inevitably changed the concept of the presiding bishop as well, did it become necessary to reformulate a role which by 1868 was already seen as venerable.

Notes

1 A fine earlier study of the collapse and reformation of the Episcopal Church is Clara O. Loveland, *The Critical Years: The Reconstitution of the Anglican Church in the United States of America: 1780-1789.* More recently Frederick V. Mills, Sr. has covered some of the ground dealt with by Dr. Loveland but has added new material on the recovery of the organization and the emerging new role of the Episcopal bishop in his *Bishops by Ballot: An Eighteenth-Century Ecclesiastical Revolution.*

2 Frederick V. Mills, Sr., *Bishops by Ballot,* pp. 160, 164. Charles R. Henery, "The Episcopal Church in Post-Revolutionary New England and New York: 1783-1811," p. 33. The phrase "suspended animation" was first used by Charles C. Tiffany, *A History of the Protestant Episcopal Church in the United States of America* (N.Y.: Scribner, 1895) and quoted with various degrees of approval by almost every historian of the Episcopal Church since.

3 The Convention of Pennsylvania, *Journal,* 1826, pp. 22-3.

4 Sydney Mead, *The Lively Experiment,* pp. 108-113.

5 John Henry Hobart, *Apology,* p. 42.

6 Chorley, *Men and Movements,* p. 182.

7 William Whittingham, "Defense of the Worship, Doctrine, and Discipline of the Church," p. 162.

8 I am indebted for this quotation to Professor J. Carleton Hayden. It is quoted in Lighton Coleman's *History of the American Church,* but its authenticity was questioned by John S. Litell in 1930. Austin Archives, 1930, General Publicty, letter to John W. Irwin. Whether authentic or not, it reflects a widely-held consensus about the Episcopal Church's conservatism.

9 Horatio Potter, *The Stability of the Church,* p. 9.

10 Concordat of November 15, 1784. One of the two originals of this Concordat is in the Library at General Theological Seminary.

11 See, for example, Canon 11 of the Canons of 1789 where confirmation and visitations were the combined responsibility of "the Bishop," "the minister," and the "church wardens."

12 *General Convention Journals from 1785 to 1853,* ed. Francis L. Hawks and W. S. Perry, vol. 1, p. 25.

13 General Convention, *Journal,* 1795, p. 207.

14 Convention of Pennsylvania, *Journal,* 1811, p. 6.

15 Convention of New York, *Journal,* 1820, pp. 12-14.

16 Convention of New Jersey, *Journal,* 1822, pp. 5-7.

17 Convention of Eastern Diocese, *Journal,* 1828, p. 3.

18 General Convention, *Journals, 1784-1814,* pp. 75-76.

19 Ibid., p. 87.

20 Ibid., pp. 122-3.

21 Ibid., pp. 152-156.

22 Ibid., p. 223.

23 Ibid., p. 186.

24 General Convention, *Journal,* 1820, p. 85.

25 Ibid., p. 52.

26 William White, "The Address of the Board of Directors of the Domestic and Foreign Missionary Society," pp. 4, 5, 9.

27 George Washington Doane, *The Path of the Just,* p. 43.

28 Bird Wilson, *Memoir of the Life of the Right Reverend William White,* p. 157.

29 *The Life and Letters of Bishop William White,* ed. Walter H. Stowe, p. 266.

30 John S. Stone, *Memoir of the Life of the Rt. Rev. Alexander Viets Griswold,* pp. 403-4.

31 General Convention, *Journal,* 1841, Constitution and Canons, p. 31.

32 *Pastoral Letter,* 1844, pp. 8-10; *Churchman,* July 6, 1843.

33 *Pastoral Letter,* 1847, p. 6.

34 General Convention, *Journal,* 1847, pp. 37, 50-51.

35 General Convention, *Journal,* 1850, pp. 127, 98, 151.

36 *Protestant Churchman,* Nov. 2, 1850: 54.

37 General Convention, *Journal,* 1850, p. 126.

38 *Guardian,* March 12, 1851, William Whittingham, "Declaration and Protest," in the Maryland Diocesan Archives; Jackson Kemper, letter dated April 30, 1851 in the Maryland Diocesan Archives.

39 Richard G. Salomon, "Philander Chase's Classified Directory of Bishops, 1844," p. 129.

40 Canons of 1979, I, II, Sec. 4, a, 1.

41 General Convention, *Journal,* 1859, p. 147.

42 Convention of Connecticut, *Journal,* 1856, p. 12.

43 General Convention, *Journal,* 1853, p. 229; 1856, p. 207.

44 General Convention, *Journal,* 1856, pp. 73-74; 1859, pp. 94, 383, 385.

45 Hopkins, *Life,* p. 343.

46 *Memorial of the Right Rev. John Henry Hopkins,* 1868, p. 14.

47 Hopkins, *Life,* p. 314.

48 *Pastoral Letter,* 1863, pp. 4, 9.

49 *Episcopal Recorder,* May 6, May 20, 1865.

50 Hopkins, *Life,* 347-8; Joseph B. Chesire, *The Church of the Confederate States,* pp. 203-204.

51 *Episcopal Recorder,* Nov. 4, 1865.

52 Actually, Hopkins, Smith, and McIlvaine were all consecrated at the same service on October 31, 1832, but Hopkins had been elected earlier and was regarded as the senior bishop.

53 Convention of Vermont, *Journal,* pp. 17-18.

54 H. C. Potter, *Reminiscences,* p. 8.

2: A National Church for a Growing Nation

The generation after Bishop Hopkins' death saw changes in the identity and character of the Episcopal Church which were almost as profound and far-reaching as those which followed the Revolutionary War. Increasingly the understanding of Episcopal identity articulated by Bishops White and Hobart became less and less adequate as the new challenges and a new understanding of this church's mission developed. The Memorialists of 1853 had asked a profoundly disturbing question. The language may be Nineteenth Century, but the question was remarkably modern. They asked

". . . whether the Protestant Episcopal Church, with only her present canonical means and appliances, her fixed and invariable modes of public worship, and her traditional customs and usages, is competent to the work of preaching and dispensing the Gospel to all sorts and conditions of men, and so adequate to do the work of the Lord in this land and in this age."

And the memorialists answered their own question:

"This question, your petitioners, for their own part, and in consonance with many thoughtful minds among us, believe must be answered in the negative."[1]

The memorialists were almost a generation ahead of their time, but by the 1870s their question could no longer be avoided. In part change was forced upon the church by challenges which were unavoidable if unwelcome. In part change came as significant spokesmen saw a new and grander vision of the destiny of this church.

The new biblical criticism and the impact of evolutionary ideas were deeply disturbing to many American Christians.[2] Episcopalians were not as easily upset by these challenges as other traditions, but they were very disturbing to many. The growth of cities and the spread of industry in areas where Episcopalians had always been numerous were also disturbing challenges. But most disturbing of all was the growth of ritualism which not only renewed the fear of Roman traitors within, but even more, challenged the uniformity and unchangeableness of liturgy which had been such a hallmark of this church. The conventions of 1868, 1871, and 1874 were dominated by ritualist conflict and resulted in the only significant schism in our history — the Reformed Episcopal Church. Bishop Smith of Kentucky might exhort his diocese in 1872 "not to make any, even the slightest innovations." No matter how unobjectionable, any change would be "sure to attract undue attention . . . to engender . . . party strife, and thus, sadly, deeply to wound our dear Lord in the house of his friends," but it was a hopeless cause.[3] The Convention of 1874 did pass an antiritual canon; but it was unenforceable. By the 1880s Horatio Potter's claim that the Episcopal Church existed "without the slightest alteration in its . . . worship" had become a hollow boast.

However, the new vision was not simply a reaction to unwelcome challenges. Some of the most distinguished and articulate Episcopalians of their day saw that the primitive and catholic claims of this church had national and ecumenical dimensions which called the Episcopal Church to a far grander mission as the national church —or at least as the basis for a national church — upon which all non-Roman Christianity could unite. It was a breathtaking vision — often expressed in chauvinistic and even racist terms, but at its best embodying a vision of a united church brought into being through the unique heritage of the Episcopal Church.

Many spokesmen developed this vision. In 1870 *The Living Church* (not the present one) saw a unique role for the Episcopal Church in the cause of unity.

". . . If we are not mistaken, the readiness for union in a Church, among all the non-Episcopal bodies of the country is very great. What is wanted is historical legitimacy, freedom of investigation and thought and study — progress in short, but connected by historical experience and tradition. In theory the Protestant Episcopal Church combines historical descent, proper respect for antiquity, with nobility and life . . . If the Protestant Episcopal Church was true to its theory it could sweep this country in twenty years, and take in all who want a positive Christian faith without falsehood or superstition."[4]

In 1890 Clarence Buel told the Episcopal Church Congress much the same:[5]

". . . One thing is very certain, and that is that there is apparently no agency so well equipped for the task of accomplishing, under God, the healing of the divisions in Christendom, as that of our own beloved church . . . even as she stands in the midst of Christendom, seemingly the only possible link which can unite its parts together on the firm basis of a restored Catholicity."

Some non-Episcopalians agreed. That bellweather of American Christianity, Henry Ward Beecher, put it this way:[6]

"Few dare to hope, and none to prophesy, that we should see advancing at last the great Episcopal Church of the United States, with her bishops, her priests, her orderly Communion, her staunch and stable men not suspected of radicalism, but rather conservative in the public estimation . . . A greater number [of people] would be willing to follow this orderly and most efficient institution than, perhaps, would be willing to follow any other leadership."

William Reed Huntington, described by his contemporaries as the most distinguished presbyter of his day, set forth in *The Church Idea* (1870) this new vision at great

37

length. And Leighton Coleman, in a consecration sermon in 1894, put the vision in its most exalted form. He emphasized the ". . . trust so providentially committed to our charge: a trust which has to do with the *molding of the spiritual life of the nation."* He was realistic enough to add this caution:[7]

> "Such a claim may provoke a smile upon the countenances of those who belong to other religious societies which at present outnumber us . . . Yet when one takes note of our growth in this respect during the past few years and now going on, one cannot but be most hopeful as to the future."

This new vision required sweeping changes in the Episcopal Church, and the last quarter of the Nineteenth Century saw those changes take place. A more flexible prayer book was needed, and the revision of 1892 was the first in our history. Comprehensiveness rather than uniformity of ritual was to be embraced, and the antiritual canon could be unanimously repealed in 1901. The Thirty-Nine Articles were too rigid for a comprehensive, national church, and Dr. Huntington set out deliberately to replace them with a new and simpler Quadrilateral which reduced "the Anglican Principle to its absolutely essential features" and thus made it "America's best hope" for union.[8] The parish house and institutional church movement, as well as the deaconness and city mission movements were efforts to expand the appeal and mission of this church to embrace all classes. The free church movement (in contrast to rented pews) was defended on the same grounds. A national church must be more unified, and the building of the Church Missions House on Fourth Avenue, New York City gave this church its first visible symbol of a national headquarters. Completed in 1894, the Church Missions House antedated the formation of the National Council by a generation.[9] Episcopal boys preparatory schools — one of the greatest achievements of this church — were now called upon to prepare Christian (and Episcopal) leaders for a Christian nation. In 1897 Bishop Potter proposed a cathedral for New York whose ". . . welcome would be for all men of whatsoever friendship, and its influence would be felt in the interests of our common Christianity throughout the whole land." The cathedrals in New York and Washington were each proclaimed as "a House of Prayer for all people."

This is not the place to develop the full story of that new ideal, but even this sketch suggests the profound change that was taking place. These new spokesmen were not primarily interested in changing the canons or the structure of government in this church. Huntington, like the Memorialists, had little interest in such change. But inevitably, a new understanding of the nature of this church would mean not only a new role for parish clergy and bishops but also changes in canons, in structure, in government, and in the long-accepted role of the presiding bishop.

* * *

One can see the first awareness of this change in the man who succeeded Hopkins as presiding bishop. In 1868 Benjamin Bosworth Smith was seventy-three years old and had been Bishop of Kentucky since 1832. He was the last surviving bishop who had been consecrated by Bishop White. The ease with which a southern bishop succeeded to the office of Presiding Bishop three years after Appomattox was an unrecorded testimony to the success of John Henry Hopkins' endeavors.

Like Brownell of Connecticut, Smith's active ministry was largely over by 1868. An assistant Bishop of Kentucky, George Cummins, had been consecrated in 1867 to assist him, and in 1869 Smith pled with the diocese to "lay aside all wrath and bitterness . . . in this, perhaps my last Address."[10] Yet he was to live for fifteen more years, dying in 1884 at the age of ninety. By then he had been a bishop for fifty-one years and presiding bishop for sixteen.

There is no major study of his life and little is actually known about him. He was a small man, weighing under 115 pounds. Early in his episcopate he had actually been brought to trial in the Diocese of Kentucky for outspoken language and forceful disagreements with others in the diocese. He was found "guilty without criminality" and restored to his office. His friend, Bishop Alfred Lee spoke of Smith's deep hurt at the time and the growing sense of moderation and caution that marked his later life.[11] By his death he was known as a "man of peace, tolerant, forebearing." Horatio Potter tells of the way he managed to avoid offense during one of the ritual issues of the day:

> "At a time when bowing at the name of Jesus in the Creed was considered as the note of an extreme school in the Church, Bishop Smith might be observed in churches in his diocese where such a usage prevailed to be in a state of gentle oscillation at the beginning of the Creed, to be increasingly so as the second article of it was reached, and, there-after, gradually to relapse into a stationary position."

He brought much of the same sense of moderation and tolerance to the House of Bishops. "In his theological and ecclesiastical views, he was [as a Southerner and evangelical] undoubtedly, during the whole period of his office as chairman of the House, in a minority. But in his recognition of those who rose to speak, and, most of all, in his appointment of committees, he was invariably just and generous."[12] Something of the same moderation can be seen in his sermon to the General Convention of 1850 on the special vocation of the Episcopal Church. The tone is moderate, traditional, and evangelical. According to Smith, this church was called to:

1. Reassert the doctrines of Grace, although those do not conflict with "the blessedness of the sacraments and

the necessity of good works."

2. Restore the Primitive Order of the Church over against "man-made Churches."

3. Bear witness to the importance of unity, which was to be "full and strict" within the Episcopal Church and "a looser compact" with other churches.

4. Revive "the true notion of the Church's care of children."

5. Bear testimony to the "principles of a just toleration upon matters of mere opinion."[13]

During his sixteen years as presiding bishop, Smith seems to have slowly become aware of the extensive responsibilities of his office. In 1868 he reported to his diocese with some amazement that he had made a trip to New York to help elect and consecrate a missionary bishop, though had he not been presiding bishop "I should have no thought, at my time of life, of undertaking" such a trip.[14] In 1872 he requested permission from the diocese to move to New York, at least until 1874. The reasons were unclear although there is no suggestion that the move was related to his office as presiding bishop. The committee which recommended approval merely referred to the request of their bishop who "at the patriarchal age of seventy-eight and for reasons of a domestic and touching interest" needed to move. Actually he stayed in Hoboken and later New York City until his death, living with his daughter and evidently making only one trip back to Kentucky in 1874. At first he rarely commented on his responsibilities as presiding bishop; but in 1874 he regularly referred to them, perhaps in part to justify his absence from the diocese. A typical report in 1876 declared that since

". . . the duties of the Presiding Bishop are increased in proportion to the rapid growth of the Church, it is almost indispensably necessary that his residence should be either in or near New York."[15]

Four years later he speculated on some possible changes

41

in the office: "The increase of duties upon the Presiding Bishop . . . are already so great as clearly to indicate that present arrangements can not much longer be continued." And he hoped that a developing provincial system would distribute those duties "among the Presiding Bishops of several Provinces, as will render non-residence of the Primus quite unnecessary."[16]

Others were also speculating. The General Conventions of 1871 and of 1874 voted Bishop Smith an expense allowance, the first such action in their history. And in 1874 a canon was actually considered which would allow the presiding bishop to resign his diocesan jurisdiction and to be supported by an assessment on each and every diocese of one dollar for each canonically resident clergyman. Convention was not ready for that, but the proposal was a sign of things to come.[17]

After all of this evidence about the increased duties of the presiding bishop, it comes as something of a shock to discover what they were. In 1884 Smith's friend and episcopal colleague, Alfred Lee, wrote a long account of his life and virtues. Lee noted that after 1874 Bishop Smith was "mainly occupied with duties as Presiding Bishop," but those duties were primarily to take order for the consecration of forty-nine bishops and to preside at sixteen of them. Although active in earlier General Conventions, ". . . for several General Conventions prior to the last, he was able to do little more than preside at the opening of each day's session of the House of Bishops and conduct the devotions."[18]

The account of his life and death in *The Churchman* simply noted that as presiding bishop he had ". . . admitted to the episcopate a larger number of bishops than it has fallen to the lot of any of his predecessors to do."[19]

Other evidence corroborates this view of Smith's activities. Although the Domestic and Foreign Missionary Society held its annual meetings in New York City, there is no evidence from the minutes that Smith attended them. Furthermore, in the thorough-going revision of the Constitution of the Missionary Society in 1877 a provision dating from 1820 which made the presiding bishop the president *ex officio* was quietly dropped.[20]

Bishop Smith's conception of his office as presiding bishop was a most traditional one: the moderate and impartial president who stands above conflict and who is primarily concerned with the consecration of bishops and with presiding at the House of Bishops. It seems likely that even Smith's interest in the development of presiding bishops of provinces was to make the work of consecrating bishops easier. Yet there were signs that changes sweeping the church were already beginning to modify this view. Residence in New York with expenses paid by General Convention were new innovations. And as the Missionary Society grew in scope and importance, the presiding bishop would not long be able to remain unrelated to that important national body.

Alfred Lee, Bishop of Delaware, succeeded as presiding bishop in 1884. He was then eighty-seven, and three years later his death brought to an end one of the shortest terms to date of that office. He presided over the House of Bishops at the Convention of 1886 and was the chief consecrator for four bishops. The Convention of 1886 revised the canon on the Missionary Society once again and restored the traditional right of the presiding bishop to be the president of the board of managers of the Society, which was now made a smaller working body of fifteen bishops, fifteen presbyters, and fifteen laymen. Bishop Lee did not attend any of the meetings of that board, but his successor did. And Lee himself was clearly interested in the cause of missions. After his death, the meeting of the Domestic and Foreign Missionary Society noted that ". . . the cause of missions lay very near his heart . . . long after the infirmities of age had begun to settle upon him, he watched the work at home and abroad, giving it counsel and guidance as occasion called."[21] However, the *Churchman,* in its eulogy, found nothing worth mentioning in his role as presiding bishop.[22] It seems likely that a man of eighty-seven played little part in the work of the office of Presiding Bishop.

* * *

John Williams, Bishop of Connecticut, who succeeded Bishop Lee in 1887, was only sixty-seven years old and a far more vigorous person. Canon Barnds, in his study of the office, believed that Bishop Williams was the first who "can truly be called the Presiding Bishop of the Protestant Episcopal Church."[23] Williams had been the much-loved president of Trinity College from 1848 to 1853, and many "old boy" stories of his activities there were passed on. He founded Berkeley Divinity School in 1854 and remained its official dean until his death in 1899. Consecrated as Bishop Coadjutor of Connecticut in 1851, he had been the bishop of that large diocese since 1865. The diocesan journals of the Diocese of Connecticut reveal a busy, energetic man deeply devoted to the work of the diocese and with little time for much else outside. In 1889 for example he conducted 121 visitations, "officiated on 180 occasions, delivered addresses 188 times, and confirmed 1,444 persons."[24] Apart from mentioning consecrations of bishops, Williams never discussed his work as presiding bishop in his reports to the Convention of Connecticut.[25]

It seems likely that his actual work as presiding bishop was limited. He presided at meetings of the Missionary Society in 1887, 1888, and again in 1894 (when the Society met in Hartford), but otherwise he was absent. His death in 1899 went virtually unnoticed in the next meeting of the Society. In 1897 Williams requested a coadjutor, and the Diocese of Connecticut in their agreement noted that ". . . his Diocese has been his first and highest interest, and while he was willing to contribute from his abundant ability to the general interests of the Church, he never failed to bear in mind his duty to the humblest Parish in his charge."[26] Indeed the *Journals* of the diocese always refer to Williams simply as the Bishop of the Diocese of Connecticut. His reports to General Convention refer to episcopal consecrations, appointing a bishop to be in charge of European congregations, etc. Perhaps the best clue to his actual work as presiding bishop can be found in a eulogy in *The Churchman:*

"The burden of the formal work attaching to the office of Presiding Bishop was little, compared with the demands made upon his attention and his time by the general work of the Church, its organized bodies and their committees, and also by appeals that were made to him to state some theological doctrine, to determine some question of ecclesiastical law, to settle some personal controversy, or to find a parish suitable for a man or a man who would be acceptable to a parish."[27]

To call Williams the first true presiding bishop may be a little misleading, if by that is meant a bishop who devotes most, or even a large proportion of his time to the work of that office. There is no evidence that Williams either gave, or was expected to give much time to the office, as it was conceived. What is true of his term, however, is that he, and the General Convention, gave more thought to the nature of the office and to possible changes in its conception than at any previous time in the history of the church.

Williams, himself, repeatedly expressed his dissatisfaction with the role. At the first meeting of the House of Bishops after his term began, he laid this message before the House:[28]

"... to lay this burden on the shoulders of the oldest Bishop of this house ... is surely something which would not be thought of in parallel cases in political, judical, or business arrangements . . . The arrangement would seem to be not only unwise, but almost cruel."

The next convention voted to allow the presiding bishop to delegate authority to an elected officer of the House, but Williams was not satisfied: "The office of Presiding Bishop is the only one of which I know, that cannot, under present arrangements, be declined," and the House again altered its rules to allow the presiding bishop to resign.[29]

But by far the most important discussion took place in the House of Deputies at the Convention of 1895. The editor of *The Churchman* described it as a "brilliant debate" and printed out the text of the addresses.[30] A thoroughgoing revision of the constitution had been proposed and passed by the House of Bishops. They presented their action to the deputies, including a provision that the presiding bishop be called the "primate." That proviso touched off a debate which lasted for several days, and examined not only the question of the name, but also the possibility of election, the meaning of the office, and its relevance to the mission of the church. Inevitably one deputy, Mr. Wilmer of Maryland, appealed to the old ideal of an unchanging church:

"It is an unspeakable comfort to feel that the Church of our fathers had never changed and never will change. . . . I appeal to you [to leave the] Church . . . as nearly as possible as it came down to us from our fathers."

But that appeal was already out of date and found little support. Many deputies were fascinated or dismayed by the proposed change of name to "primate." Several pointed out the power of a name in, I think, a remarkably perceptive way. Dr. Green of New York told the deputies

"Names have something more than an etymological signification . . . In a name that is full of ancient and memorable association a whole history . . . is sometimes instantaneously disclosed . . . There is great power in nomenclature, because there is history in it. There is more power, I think, in nomenclature than there is in legislation. Give me the right to select the historic name for a system or institution, and anyone who chooses may have the right to formulate its laws."

Others emphasized the power of the term "primate" to identify us with the rest of the Anglican Communion. Dr. Green of Iowa declared, "I shall welcome this term 'primate,' because it put us into touch with that Anglican Christianity, to which we owe all that we are."

Others agreed about the power of the name, but feared that it would alienate an American culture and harm the growing mission of the church. Dr. Elliott of Maryland said, "We are very fond of calling ourselves the American Church. . . Let us then be American in our terms . . . Let us take names which are easily interpreted by the people among whom we live." And he finished with a flourish:

"It is the simplicity of Bethlehem and not the splendor of Jerusalem which will give us victory over the hearts of the American people."

Others saw the change of name as pretentious, considering the insignificance of the duties of the office. Dr. Harwood of Connecticut (whose bishop was the presiding bishop) said,

"He is a Primate in name, not in fact. He has no provincials; he has no court; he has no power. He has nothing to add influence to the position, and yet you call him a Primate."

The Rev. Mr. Weller of Fond du Lac noted that the position was "largely an honorary" one, but the Rev. Mr. Edmunds of Albany used much stronger language:

"The Presiding Bishop is hardly more than a clerical officer and his work hardly more than that of a clerk . . . Of course it is an honor to be a servant of the Church . . . but the office of Presiding Bishop was

47

not created, and does not now exist, for the purpose of bestowing honor upon any bishop. The office exists for the purpose of doing certain work."

and he recommended that an elected presiding bishop would get the work done more efficiently.

Easily the most distinguished defense of the term "primate" came from Dr. Huntington of New York. He was not interested in terms like "archbishop" or "metropolitan" because they were hierarchical." But the term "primate" was valuable because it associated the office with ". . . the venerableness of old age, and I submit that veneration for old age is one of the primary principles of Christian morals." And when another deputy argued that the oldest bishop could not be very active, Huntington replied at once:

"We do not want the Primate to be too active. We want the office to be an honorary one and to mark all that accompanies old age."

But already the question had shifted from that of the name to the possibility of an elected presiding bishop. In language that was a portent of the future, the Rev. Mr. Fitts of Alabama introduced images that would soon be familiar.

"I do not presume there is a lay deputy in this House who would take stock in any company . . . whose president was elected by virtue of seniority; and I do not see why, in building up the Church in America, where the head is chosen, we should adopt a role against which we are constantly acting in all our worldly affairs."

And when it was objected that the House of Bishops had the right to choose and name their presiding officer as they wished, Dr. Mann of Missouri also spoke for the future:

"The Presiding Bishop is not simply the Presiding Bishop of the House of Bishops but he is the Presiding Bishop of this whole church."

As such he should be elected, and the House of Deputies should participate in that election. Within six years, the first effort would be made to write that provision into the canons.

In the end the deputies decided to leave the term "presiding bishop" intact.[31] But a debate of this depth and length, engaging some of the leading speakers in the church was a sign of new interest and a desire to reexamine an office that had largely grown with little forethought.

Williams himself presided at the House in a classic manner. Bishop Potter described his role in admirable terms:[32]

"When he presided in the House, his regard for the Rules of Order was most scrupulous; and one never knew, unless one chose to infer it from previous associations . . . on which side of any particular question were his personal sympathies. In a word he was a most impartial presiding officer; never a partisan, never a limp creature of the impulse of the moment, courteous but firm; and amid the confusions of debate often bringing order out of chaos by a few unimpassioned but illuminating sentences."

When he died at the age of eighty-two, he was again the senior bishop in the Anglican Communion.

*   *   *

His successor, Thomas March Clark, was eighty-six in 1899. He had been Bishop of Rhode Island since 1854. He was to be presiding bishop for only three years, and was unable to attend any meeting of the House of Bishops during his term. Yet his term was significant. During it efforts were made to cope with changes in the office of Presiding Bishop; Thomas Clark did much to encourage those efforts. As *The Churchman* editorialized after his death, "The significance of his administration as Presiding

Bishop has not yet been fully realized and will not be till the Church more fully realizes herself as a National Church."[33]

Bishop Clark's *Reminiscences* reveal a person of considerable wit, charm, and curiosity. His daughter wrote that he

". . . had long felt very strongly that, as the Church had so greatly increased in numbers and strength, this position, which now had become one of great responsibility, should be held by a bishop selected for his special qualifications for the office and one in middle life."[34]

Like some of his predecessors, Clark seems to have discovered that the office involved more work and responsibility than he suspected at first. "I had supposed," he wrote, "when the office came to me, that its duties were few and simple, but a glance at the Record Book will show how much I mistook the situation, for its responsibilities have involved much labor and anxiety."[35] And Clark went on to detail responsibilities beyond those of presiding and taking order for consecrations.

"There is the responsibility of the appointment of provisional bishops and, in case of vacancies as in Mexico at the present moment, the care of the church in this [i.e., that] country. There is the duty of calling special meetings of the House of Bishops and, under certain circumstances, the responsibility of deciding the time and place for the meetings of the General Convention. There is the calling together of councils of conciliation, and the Presiding Bishop is the representative of the Church in America in its correspondence with foreign countries."[36]

For a busy diocesan bishop, whose main responsibility was his own diocese, and who was usually a few years away from death, that was quite a bit.

At one point Bishop Clark was involved in controversy over his office when he protested at the ritualism of a consecration in Fond du Lac. His daughter gives the best account of his reaction:[37]

"He asserted himself, perhaps a little too sternly, on the occasion of a consecration in which additions of which he did not approve were made to the usual service, and received from the bishops who took part a very severe reprimand. Never before, it was said, had a Presiding Bishop been such an autocrat or presumed so much upon his official position; and a remonstrance, drawn up by seven bishops, was sent to him."

He was especially criticized for calling himself "Presiding Bishop of the Church." Bishop Clark laughed about the whole matter, met with the bishops, and later wrote, "I had not even noticed that I called myself 'Presiding Bishop of the Church' until my attention was called to it by the newspapers, though, taking into consideration all that had to be done for the Church at large in this office, there might be sufficient reason for the title."[38]

The most significant action of his term, however, took place at the General Convention of 1901 which met in San Francisco. Clark was not present, but his address, read early in the convention, clearly struck a responsive chord. He told the convention that there are "certain important things which the Presiding Bishop is required to do which call for the exercise of careful judgment and great discretion" and he urged the convention to make "the office of Presiding Bishop elective, instead of leaving it to be determined by the simple fact of seniority." And then in words that were to be prophetic, he called attention to the need to define the nature of the office more carefully:[39]

"There is nowhere to be found any general statement whatever of the duties pertaining to the office, and as it requires a careful examination of the Canons in order to ascertain just what it is that the Presiding Bishop is called upon to do, may I be allowed to suggest that some statement should be set forth clearly defining the functions and duties of the office."

A major debate in the House of Deputies took place on October 3rd. One description of the scene may help remind us that the convention was not always orderly nor the debate profound. As the debate began, one correspondent noted that "protests began to come in . . . that proceedings were inaudible, while a desultory discussion of remedies . . . consumed much time and effected little . . . The evil is . . . due chiefly to disorder." Nonetheless, there was a recognition that an important matter was under consideration. The correspondent for *The Living Church* reported that, "The change from Presiding Bishop of the House of Bishops to Presiding Bishop of the Church was repeatedly pointed out as a radical one" and the reporter from *The Churchman* added that ". . . the opinion of the House was clearly against appointment by seniority, which had also been condemned by Bishop Clark in his report to the bishops, read this morning."[40]

There was considerable negotiation between the houses, and an amendment to the Constitution was finally passed which provided for the election of "the Presiding Bishop of the Church" by the House of Bishops with confirmation by the House of Deputies. He was to hold office for three years. A discussion of his duties was postponed for later action.[41]

As we will see, this constitutional amendment failed to pass in 1904 and thus died, but the conception of the office as envisaged in 1901 is worth some examination. There was no suggestion that the elected presiding bishop could cease to be a diocesan bishop; indeed a term of three years suggested a rotating office. The method of selection — election by the House of Bishops, confirmation by the House of Deputies — was to be the final solution chosen by the Church. Even more significant was the embryonic sense that a new understanding of the office was required. The editor of *The Churchman* expressed that new concept clearly; a national church needs a national leader.

> "The democracy of the Church demands that the whole body shall have its representative and the efficiency of the Church as an organization equally demands a chief executive. We trust that Bishop Clark's administration is prophetic of an aggressive development toward a more effective and more representative organization."[42]

"A chief executive" — the debate was now fairly joined; and in the next two decades, a decision would be made.

*   *   *

Thomas Clark's death brought to the office of Presiding Bishop one of its more colorful and vigorous occupants. Daniel Sylvester Tuttle had been consecrated Missionary Bishop of Montana, Idaho, and Utah in 1867 when he was thirty; in 1903 he was only sixty-six years old and had been Bishop of Missouri since 1886. He was to be presiding bishop for twenty years, and by his death in 1923 the most important canonical change in the history of that office had taken place.

Bishop Tuttle was a colorful person. *The Churchman* printed many magnificent photographs of this tall, venerable, imposing man with a full, white beard. Two tributes from two very different persons capture something of the vitality and humanness of Tuttle. The first is from Bitter Root Bill, "a noted desperado:"[43]

> "He's a better man than Joe Floweree; he's the biggest and best bishop that ever wore a black gown . . . He's full jeweled and eighteen karats fine. . . . He's a fire fighter from away back, and whenever he chooses to go [on] a brimstone raid among the sinners in this gulch, he can do it, and I'll back him with my pile."

Edward L. Parsons, the retired Bishop of California, wrote a gentler tribute:[44]

"He wrote his sermons, he took regular exercise. He tithed to be sure that he gave rightly to the Lord's work . . . He was adventurous, generous, outgoing and outgiving, warm-hearted, emotional, breaking into tears, touched by need and sorrow and by sin."

Such was the man who, among other things, took order for the consecrations of one hundred and twelve bishops and personally presided at the consecration of eighty. Clearly, a new man was on the job!

The General Convention which met in Trinity Church, Boston in 1904 faced the question of confirming the constitutional changes proposed three years earlier, making the office of Presiding Bishop a three-year elective one. Even the church press was interested. Shortly before Convention met, a lay deputy from Kentucky, Mr. W. A. Robinson had proposed an even more sweeping canon which would allow the presiding bishop to remain in office until he was seventy, and more important, would require him to function solely as presiding bishop with his support for life coming from funds of the General Convention. *The Churchman* supported the proposal: "The need of a Chief Executive is widely felt . . . It is wholly within our power to have a representative Chief Executive for the Church, who, because he is representative, will accomplish greater things." The visit of Archbishop Davidson of Canterbury to Boston aroused much interest, and several thought the American church should have a real counterpart.[44]

Mr. Robinson presented his canon to the convention, and a flurry of legislative activity followed. It was a carefully thought out canon, and Mr. Robinson presented it with vigor. Eventually the proposal received an equally distinguished reply from none other than William Reed Huntington, Chairman of the Committee on the Constitution. Huntington noted that the presiding bishop had a mixture of duties, "partly ministerial, partly ceremonial, and partly executive." But, he added, "it does not appear to your committee that the duties thus classified are sufficiently onerous to justify so wide a departure from our present usage." And he noted that the Archbishop of Canterbury himself found time to be bishop of a diocese as well as Primate of All England. Then turning to more weighty reasons, he spoke from his own understanding of the future he hoped for this church, a future which had little to do with legislative or executive efficiency:

"It has been urged . . . that the Episcopal Church in this country needs a formal mouth-piece through which to utter itself . . . upon questions of this day . . . but it may be gravely questioned whether the authority to commit the Church, as a whole, to any given belief or policy would wisely or safely be entrusted to an individual, however exalted his official position might be. *Ex cathedra* utterances might land us . . . in ecclesiastical imperialism."

Significantly, Huntington did note one contingency which might make a full-time presiding bishop necessary: "Were responsible executive functions ever to be assigned to the President of the Domestic and Foreign Missionary Society, functions so various and exacting as to require for their discharge the undivided attention of the holder of the office, it might then become desirable" to make the change. In the meantime, more "stenographers and typewriters" and a raise in the presiding bishop's expense account should suffice.[46]

At the same time the House of Bishops turned to the question of ratification of the 1901 constitutional change. All meetings of the House of Bishops were closed, and there is no report of the debate. The record simply records that the bishops did not concur. It seems likely that the presence of a new presiding bishop who, in 1911 was still described as "vigorous and lion-hearted beyond most younger men"[47] made the question of a rotating presiding bishop seem very different than it had three years earlier when Thomas Clark was the absent and aged senior bishop. And although I have found no record of any opinion expressed by Bishop Tuttle in 1904, his opposition to the change was later to be well-known and certainly public.

But the House of Deputies was not content to let the matter drop, and Mr. Robinson persuaded his House to insist on a joint committee to prepare recommendations for the next Convention. The bishops agreed.[48] The last word came from *The Churchman,* after the Convention was over. They, too, would not let the matter drop.

"A representative and administrative head is as essential to the unity of purpose as to the unity of action of the American Church. From the standpoint of utility, the need of such an executive is a pressing necessity. . . . Common sense and common justice cry out."[49]

The next two Conventions witnessed continued maneuvers. Both houses again adopted in 1907 a constitutional amendment providing for a rotating elected presiding bishop but the House of Bishops insisted on modifying the proposal in 1910, thus postponing action once more until 1913. The Convention which met in New York City that year saw the last major debate on the nature of the office before the great changes of 1919.

Before the Convention began, the Rev. Thomas L. Cole stated clearly the new view, an ideal which lay behind Mr. Robinson's proposal and an ideal which would largely be written into the canons in 1919. Mr. Cole saw clearly the significance of the change:

"The change in the method of appointing the Presiding Bishop has in view a change in the character of the office itself, the creation of a strong executive head for the Church."

Cole appealed to executive-type images in support of his expressed view:

"Aggressive military campaigning, successful corporate business operations, effective civil government, none of these are accomplished without leadership, without a head . . . The verdict of history was for the primate."

He concluded with the strongest argument yet advanced: a national church must have a national leader. This church ". . . cannot have commanding influence, or offer effective service in the constitution of a comprehensive and truly national church unless he is a 'real President Bishop.' "[50]

By now most of the positions had been fully stated and it remained only for the conservative position, which looked back to an earlier ideal, to be forcefully presented. It was so presented in 1913 and by the distinguished presiding bishop himself — Daniel Tuttle. Tuttle's arguments have sometimes been dismissed as hopelessly backward looking, but they deserve more respect. He clearly saw the nature of the changes which were proposed (and which would come into effect only after his death) and he did not like them at all.

He first dealt with the question of efficiency. If an efficient presiding officer of the House of Bishops is all that is needed, the present system of choosing an assistant or assessor who could do the work of presiding would suffice. (It was, in fact, the system that Bishop Tuttle himself used.) But the question, he saw, was not that of making the present office more efficient but of changing the office itself. Tuttle broke with tradition by publishing his objections publicly.[51]

"The proposed change is significant of contemplated changes in the powers and duties of the Presiding Bishop. Now, such powers and duties are ministerial rather than executive . . . The proposed change has in view the making of the Presiding Bishop into a great executive, to be invested with the authority and to be deputed to wield the powers of the whole church . . . Danger lurks along this line of development . . . The proposed change looks to the introducing of a monarchial plan for our national church which in time might take on a Hildebrandian touch and tone."

By now three clearly different views of the office have been set forth. Tuttle spoke for the past, for an office which was indeed largely ministerial, concerned with consecrations, with meetings of the House, and with a minor number of administrative matters which were nonetheless growing. An impartial presiding office, a symbolic figure, but in no real sense a chief executive officer, was his vision.

William Reed Huntington took second place to none in his concern for the church's forward and relevant mission. His view was a large one of a church united by a common faith and a fundamental worship. For him, however, legislative and canonical matters could, if pressed, only hurt that larger unity. Even more than Tucker, he wanted a presiding bishop who was a venerable patriarch, a symbol of the unity for which he worked so hard. After all, as he said, "we do not want the Primate to be too active."

But the Episcopal Church always had a difficult time grappling with Huntington's vision,[52] and the view set forth so clearly by Robinson and Cole was, perhaps inevitably, to win the day. Centralization was the movement of the times; the First World War showed clearly and devastingly the powers that centralization could mobilize, and if the church was to mobilize, a chief executive officer was needed. Who else could that be except the presiding bishop? Cole had written, "The *primus inter pares* . . .[view] cannot stand the test of either history or reason . . . the time shall come . . . for a real President Bishop."[53] "What the Church wants is an efficient executive, and nothing less than that."[54]

Surprisingly, one note which will become prominent in

the mid-twentieth century was absent from this date (or mentioned, only to be rejected on all sides). There was no suggestion that the presiding bishop was in any way expected to be a unique or especially significant witness to God's word or to act in a uniquely prophetic role. Nor was the term "chief pastor" or any equivalent used by those who wanted to set forth a new ideal of that office. In 1913 the new role clearly placed major emphasis on administrative and executive duties — a more efficient church, a church called to national leadership, required a more efficient and effective "chief executive officer." In supporting the change in the Constitution, a *Living Church* editorial argued that ". . . the executive head should be made an efficient factor and not an ornamental appendix to our ecclesiastical system."[55]

In the end, the Convention of 1913 anticlimactically voted the constitutional change down; or rather, the bishops did. *The Churchman* suggested their reasons for doing so. Although technical ambiguities were cited,

". . . it is plain . . . that the bishops do not desire an elected Presiding Bishop with large powers. Many who voted against the proposition as it came up for final action are said to approve the principle and to be ready to vote for a well-guarded provision to elect the Presiding Bishop and limit his powers."[56]

Concern for centralization and efficiency must be seen in terms of the early twentieth century and not in terms of contemporary suspicion of bureaucracy. In the early part of this century churches everywhere used the language of efficient business and centralization but almost always in relation to the mission of the church. Because mission, especially world-wide mission, was enthusiastically supported, the call came for efficient centralization. The implicit (and often explicit) assumption underlying the idea of the presiding bishop as chief executive officer was the assumption that the major work of the national church was that of mission. An editorial in *The Living*

Church put the point clearly:[57]

> "The principle that must essentially be realized is
> that the Presiding Bishop must be intimately related
> to the Missionary Society, so that all missionary
> work be made directly under the chief care of the
> Church itself."

Those who were concerned for a more centralized and
efficient mission soon began to look far beyond the office
of Presiding Bishop. Indeed nothing less than a thorough
reorganization of the entire on-going national work of
this church had to be undertaken. Initial impetus came
from the Domestic and Foreign Missionary Society.
That Society had been reorganized in 1920, and Arthur S.
Lloyd, who had been general secretary of the Society since
1899 was made the new president. Lloyd was now Bishop
of Virginia and the leading spirit in developing a new,
integrated structure for carrying out the mission of the
church. For our purposes the most singificant action of
the 1913 Convention was probably not its refusal to
authorize an elected presiding bishop, but its approval,
on the initiative of the Board of Missions, to create a joint
commission ". . . to investigate and reconsider the whole
question of Missionary Organization and Administration,
and to report to the next General Convention." Although
that commission presented an extensive report to the
Convention of 1916, little could be done. The United
States was approaching our first great international war;
feelings were running high. It was not a good time to
consider a drastic revision of church structure. But the
Convention of 1916 did make one significant change in
the canon on the Missionary Society — a canon which
contained in embryo the idea of a national program and
budget.[58]

> "At the General Convention of 1919, and at each
> subsequent Convention, the Board of Missions shall
> submit a budget for the ensuing year, and a provi-
> sional estimate for each of the succeeding two years.

The budget and estimate and the report of the Board of Missions hereinafter required, shall be considered by the two Houses of General Convention in Joint Session assembled."

Also in 1916 a final version of a constitutional change was passed which called for an elected presiding bishop, whose term of office and duties would be determined by canon. He would be elected by the House of Bishops and confirmed by the House of Deputies. The provision would not become final until 1919, but the 1916 text was eventually to be approved.

The years 1916 and 1919 were momentous ones for this country. World War I plunged the entire western world into its greatest international agony in centuries. The United States declared war in April, 1917; by November, 1918 the war was over and won. 1919 was a heady year. If a military victory was possible, what might not the church of Christ do? It is amazing that the popular, national movement known as "The Nation-Wide Movement" should have been conceived and have aroused such enthusiasm and commitment within a few months. In 1919 the movement to make the presiding bishop an elected, full-time "chief executive officer," to create a unified, ongoing national body — known in 1919 as the Presiding Bishop and Council — and to see all this within the context of a renewed commitment to the mission of this church came to fruition between February and October. There were, of course, many precedents for all three movements and much had gone on to prepare the way. But seldom had such major changes been carried through in so few weeks.

It was "The Nation-Wide Movement" that caught the imagination of the church. At a fateful meeting of the Board of Missions on February 12, 1919 the Board took two actions which were to bear much fruit. The Board first approved a resolution calling for a national reawakening to mission.

"It is the sense of the Board of Missions that a nationwide campaign of missionary information, education and inspiration should be begun at the first possible moment."

At the same meeting the Board approved a proposal to plan for the creation of "an Executive Board for the General Convention" which would unite three independent boards: the Board of Missions, the General Board of Religious Education, and the Joint Commission on Social Service.[59]

The "Nation-Wide Movement" attracted much more public interest. Committees were formed, speeches and articles written, a slogan adopted ("To inform the mind and awaken the conscience"), and meetings held. *The Southern Church* expressed strong approval and *The Living Church* made its October 4th issues a Nation-Wide Campaign issue. The editor, Frederick Cook Morehouse, caught the spirit of the movement in an editorial.[60]

"The Nation-wide Campaign is the center of interest. For it there is splendid enthusiasm. It appeals to the *imagination* of Churchmen. We are ashamed to be petty in this day of great things, when God is making all things new."

At the same time progress was being made in plans for a unified executive board. A joint committee released a report on June 15, 1919 calling for an executive board composed of seventy-six members! The report was approved by all three independent boards which would be united by the proposed canon.

The Convention of 1919 met in Detroit, joint meetings being held in a somewhat bizarre dance hall, Arcadia Hall. Expectations of changes and new directions were in the air. The indefatigable president of the Board of Missions and the leading spirit behind the plan for a unified council, Bishop Arthur Selden Lloyd, wrote just before the Convention began,

"This Convention will probably be a turning point in the history of the American Church."

Charles Henry Brent, Bishop of the Philippines and Chief of Chaplains during the war, gave the opening sermon. Every major church paper reprinted that electric sermon which rang changes again and again on the new opportunities that awaited the church.[61]

"The new era is upon us. It began in international affairs and its spirit must be given cordial hospitality in domestic affairs. The truth and justice and honor and liberty which the war has hewn free cannot be allowed to rest until they have found permanent lodging in every department of human life, at home and abroad."

One witness wrote later of the impact of that sermon on all who were present:[62]

"Judging from the enthusiasm shown by comments made afterward the convention was ready to take somewhat drastic measures to set the Church to her task in meeting the problems of today as outlined by Bishop Brent."

One quietly dramatic sign of a new era was the ease with which the House of Bishops dropped a 130-year rule that their meetings would be closed. The call to end secret meetings had been issued many times; in 1919 the time had come. As one prominent deputy, Walter Russel Bowie, put it, "The news that the old policy had been reversed was of exceptional importance in its effect upon the whole atmosphere of the Convention."[63]

For the 538 deputies who met in Arcadia Hall, a sense of surprise, newness and excitement seemed to break into the meetings again and again. Here is an extraordinary account by an unnamed reporter who was rather mechanically recording the events of the day:[64]

"I had received advance copies of the speeches, and so about the middle of the afternoon my mind began to wander . . .

"Suddenly I was awakened, as by the sound of a mighty, rushing voice. Something was happening that was not on the programme. Dr. Freeman, the presiding officer, began to make an impromptu speech. In ten short minutes he was giving us his great vision of the mission of the American Church. I forgot about my press material. I forgot about sleep. I lost sight of comfort and self, for I knew that the most masterful speech of the Convention was being made. I do not remember all that was said, for I forgot to take notes. I only remembered the final words, "As for the result of the Nation-wide Campaign, I have too much faith in Him, whom I left my former position to serve, to doubt the final issue."

"And then, for the first time during any session of the Convention in Arcadia Hall, the whole House got down on its knees and prayed."

The deputies and bishops in Detroit who put together canons that brought an elected "Presiding Bishop and Council" into being were certainly not afraid of corporate, executive, and bureaucratic images. But to see the new "Presiding Bishop and Council" simply in canonical and administrative terms is to miss the exciting dynamic that was the reason for the change. The leaders at the Detroit Convention saw an elected "Presiding Bishop and Council" as the obvious, effective, and efficient way to strengthen the mission of the church. If one thing is clear from the dusty pages of the records of the 1919 Convention, it is that a new vision of that mission was the overwhelming motivation behind the drastic changes in national structure which were made then.

And changes in structure there were. The Constitutional amendment approved first in 1916 received final approval and became part of the constitution. The presiding bishop would be elected by the House of Bishops and confirmed by the House of Deputies. His term and duties would be defined by canon. He was still expected to retain his diocesan jurisidiction as well, and would cease to be presiding bishop if he resigned as diocesan.

More debate took place about the appropriate canon. An executive board of seventy-six members (as proposed by an interim committee) hardly seemed the efficient structure that was needed, and the House of Deputies modified the proposal considerably. It seems likely that Mr. George Zabriskie was the leading figure in writing the new canon. At least, so the reporter for *The Churchman* thought.[65]

"Mr. George Zabriskie is also the author of the canon providing for the Presiding Bishop and Council. His plan won among the various schemes presented; and, because he had thought out the plan in detail, it held against criticism . . . It will be safe to say that by his clear and constructive thought Mr. George Zabriskie was the outstanding leader of the General Convention of 1919."

Canon 60 called for an executive board of twenty-four members. Sixteen members of the Council were to be elected by the General Convention and eight by the Provincial Synods. The charter of the new board was written into the first sentence of the canon:[66]

"The Presiding Bishop and Council, as hereinafter constituted, shall administer and carry on the Missionary, Educational and Social Work of the Church, of which work the Presiding Bishop shall be the executive head."

The Council was organized into five departments: Missions and Church Extension, Religious Education, Christian Social Service, Finance, and Publicity. The Council could organize other departments if need arose.[67]

Canon 60 fixed the term of office of the Presiding Bishop at six years. Article II repeated the two most traditional duties of that office: He ". . . shall preside over meetings of the House of Bishops, and shall take order for the consecration of Bishops." The new ideal was soberly enshrined in the rest of that article for the first time in this church's history: "He shall be the executive head of all departments of the Church's work, including those of Missions and Church Extension, of Religious Education and of Christian Social Service."[68]

A presiding bishop was not to be elected until the office became vacant. Bishop Tuttle was then eighty-two though he was to live until 1923. Canon 60 provided an interim arrangement whereby another bishop woud be elected as president of the Council until a new presiding bishop was chosen. Many expected Bishop Lloyd to be chosen, but in fact the Right Rev. Thomas Frank Gailor, Bishop of Tennessee, was elected. Within a few months the council was organized; their first report in 1920 noted that income for the mission of the church had about doubled within the year.

When the Convention adjourned on October 24th, it closed a memorable era in this church's history. Even after the excitement had died down, the conviction remained that some epoch-making steps had taken place. Bishop E. L. Parsons gave a sober and considered estimate of its achievements:[69]

"The national council with the Presiding Bishop at its head revolutionizes our whole church life and work. It makes a compact and effective organization instead of a group of unrelated boards. It gives a head with real executive power . . . The legislation was very hastily done. There is too great centralization to represent the whole Church and too little concentration of responsibility for the best executive action. But the gain is enormous and details can be worked out as the years go by."

There was surprisingly little opposition to the whole change, both during and after the Convention. Bishop Sessums of Louisiana did ask ". . . if the ancient rights and liberties of the bishops and dioceses were sufficiently guarded" and Bishop Weller of Fond du Lac objected to "swallowing the pill whole." It was, he said, "the most revolutionary measure ever presented."[70] Even *The Churchman* was a little uneasy:

"We confess to our being suspicious of centralization . . . The powers entrusted to this commission seem to us to involve the setting up of what amounts to a curia."

But *The Churchman* concluded with a vote of confidence that was remarkably perceptive:[71]

"We believe in centralization. It is the tendency of the hour. The war has taught us the surrender of a certain individualism in the interest of an authority which can function efficiently. But the war has also taught us that any centralization which does not find a quick current passing from centre to circumference leads to an irresponsible absolutism."

And *The Living Church* was also enthusiastic: "The most important piece of legislation that the American Church has even enacted was formally made a law of the Church last week in Detroit by the General Convention" and three weeks later the same periodical concluded with this judgment:[72]

"The outstanding achievements of the General Convention in Detroit are profoundly impressive. It is too early to make absolute comparisons, and yet one cannot escape the well nigh universal impression that the Convention of 1919 will prove to be the most eventful that the Church has ever known."

Subsequent commentators have been equally positive. Dr. Edwin A. White, one of the great canonists of this church, wrote in 1924 that Canon 60

". . . undoubtedly marks a greater change in the polity of the American Church than any other Canon ever enacted by General Convention, and is one of the greatest pieces of constructive legislation, if not the greatest, ever enacted by that body since the first General Council of 1789."[73]

In 1952 Dr. C. Rankin Barnes, then secretary of both the House of Deputies and the National Council, wrote that the General Convention of 1919 ". . . has definitely taken its place as the most important held in this century and as one of the most important ever held."[74]

Bishop Edward Parsons had noted that some details would need to be worked out in the years ahead. That was true, and a good deal of time would be spent as the full implications of the change became clearer. In fact the questions would go much deeper. Article Two of Canon 60 really put two different conceptions of the office of Presiding Bishop side by side. The older view of a presiding officer and sacramental figure standing above conflict and symbolizing the national character of this church was simply combined with a very different view of an executive officer concerned with administration of the church's mission and — at least in principle — expected to take decided stands and to support distinctive programs and ventures. I have not found any awareness of this implicit tension by those who made the change; only time was to make that tension more evident. Nor was it possible in 1919 to ask whether this new view of the presiding bishop was in fact an adequate and satisfying one for the whole church. Those questions lay in the future.

Finally, the importance of canonical changes should not be overemphasized. Undoubtedly far more revolutionary changes took place in the late nineteenth century when this church's understanding of its identity and its mission were altered dramatically. By 1919 that vision of a national church was itself undergoing modification —the image of the "bridge church" was beginning to be popular. Those changes affected vastly more Episcopalians than any changes in national structure. Indeed the changes in structure were themselves reflections of a deeper change in self-identity. But once all those cautions have been made, the legislation of 1919 does stand out as especially significant, not least for the role of the presiding bishop. An older, classic view had been significantly altered, and a conception of the presiding bishop which is still fundamentally operative had been enthusiastically written into the canons and, more important, into the national life of the church.

Notes

1 The Memorial Papers, p. 28
2 See, for example, Paul A. Carter's *The Spiritual Crisis of the Gilded Age,* 1971.
3 Convention of Kentucky, *Journal,* 1872, p. 35.
4 *The Living Church,* April, 1870: 187.
5 Episcopal Church Congress, 1890, p. 46.
6 *The Churchman,* 1884: 262.
7 Leighton Coleman, *Our Ecclesiastical Heritage,* pp. 5, 10 (Emphasis added).
8 William Reed Huntington, *Church Idea,* p. 125.
9 There is an account by Julia C. Emery, *A Century of Endeavor: 1821-1921,* pp. 220-3.
10 Convention of Kentucky, *Journal,* 1869, pp. 34-35.
11 See the account of his trial which took place in 1837 by W. Robert Insko, "The Trial of a Kentucky Bishop," General Theological Seminary pamphlet collection. Bishop Lee's address is in the Convention of Kentucky, *Journal,* 1884, pp. 58-73.
12 Potter, *Reminiscences,* p. 11.
13 B. B. Smith, *Special Vocation of the Protestant Episcopal Church.*
14 Convention of Kentucky, *Journal,* 1868, p. 26.
15 Ibid., 1876, p. 43.
16 Ibid., 1878, p. 58.
17 General Convention, *Journal,* 1874, pp. 40, 91.
18 Convention of Kentucky, *Journal,* 1884, p. 72.
19 *The Churchman,* June 7, 1884: 620.
20 White and Dykman, *Annotated Constitution and Canons,* I:190-1.
21 Proceedings of the Domestic and Foreign Missionary Society, 1887, p. 13.
22 *The Churchman,* April 23, 1887: 475.
23 W. J. Barnds, "The Office of the Presiding Bishop," p. 268.
24 Convention of Connecticut, *Journal,* 1889, pp. 29-31.
25 For accounts of consecrations, see Convention of Connecticut, *Journal,* 1890, p. 37; 1891, p. 46.
26 Convention of Connecticut, *Journal,* 1897, p. 51.
27 *The Churchman,* February 18, 1899: 261.
28 General Convention, *Journal,* 1889, p. 538.
29 Ibid., 1892, pp. 12, 88.
30 See *The Churchman,* October 19 and October 26, 1895.
31 General Convention, *Journal,* 1895, pp. 226, 272-2.
32 Potter, *Reminiscences,* pp. 33-4.
33 *The Churchman,* September 19, 1903: 317.
34 Mary Clark Sturtevant, *Thomas March Clark,* p. 159.
35 Ibid., pp. 160-1.
36 Ibid.
37 Ibid., p. 160
38 Ibid.

[39] General Convention, *Journal,* 1901, pp. 15-16.
[40] *The Living Church,* October 12, 1901: 799; *The Churchman,* October 12, 1901: 473.
[41] General Convention, *Journal,* 1901, pp. 27, 40-41, 54, 55, 139, 148, 151, 211, 223-4, 263, 300, 307,. 310.
[42] *The Churchman,* September 19, 1903: 317.
[43] Ibid., October 7, 1916: 470.
[44] Edward L. Parsons, "Bishop Tuttle — A Portrait," p. 147.
[45] *The Churchman,* October 8, 1904:
[46] General Convention, *Jouirnal,* 1904, p. 265.
[47] Julia C. Emery, *A Century of Endeavor,* p. 269.
[48] General Convention, *Journal,* 1904, pp. 211, 232, 265.
[49] *The Churchman,* November 19, 1904: 913-4.
[50] Ibid., October 4, 1913: 447-8.
[51] Ibid., August 23, 1913: 243.
[52] See, for example, the extended debate about the "Huntington amendment" on church unity in the Conventions of 1901 and 1904.
[53] *The Churchman,* October 4, 1913: 447-8.
[54] *The Living Church,* October 18, 1913: 847.
[55] Ibid., August 9, 1913: 515.
[56] *The Churchman,* October 25, 1913: 558.
[57] *The Living Church,* October 18, 1913: 847.
[58] General Convention, *Journal,* 1916, pp. 147-8.
[59] Emery, *Century of Endeavor,* p. 320.
[60] *The Living Church,* October 18, 1919: 873.
[61] Ibid., October 11, 1919: 840-2; *The Churchman,* October 25, 1919: 22-23.
[62] *The Churchman,* October 25, 1919: 21.
[63] *The Southern Churchman,* October 18, 1919: 4.
[64] *The Living Church,* October 25, 1919: 911.
[65] *The Churchman,* November 15, 1919: 21.
[66] General Convention, *Journal,* 1919, p. 412.
[67] Ibid., pp. 154-162.
[68] Ibid., Constitution and Canons, p. 65.
[69] *The Churchman,* November 15, 1919: 14.
[70] Ibid.: 12.
[71] Ibid., August 23, 1919: 7.
[72] *The Living Church,* November 1, 1919: 19; November 22, 1919: 110.
[73] Edwin A. White, *Constitution and Canons, Annotated,* p. 958. The same comment was retained by Jackson A. Dykman in his revision of White's commentary, *Annotated Constitution and Canons,* I:244.
[74] C. Rankin Barnes, "The General Convention of 1919," p. 250.

3: The Presiding Bishop of the Church

Images are, in many ways, very revealing. In this investigation they have been one of the best ways of finding a deeper understanding of the role of the presiding bishop. Images have a cluster of meanings, partly intellectual and party affective, which determine not only canons and administrative procedures but also the ways in which a presiding bishop is seen and the expectations placed upon him. To move from the image of the venerable patriarch to that of the corporate chief executive was to make a profound change. Much of the rest of the twentieth century would be spent in reflecting on that change. Most striking was the unwillingness to be content with the image of chief executive officer. By the time the first presiding bishop was actually elected in 1925, the image had already been subtly modified.

Change is rarely total. Older understandings continue to exert influence and to live within or at least along with the new. One dramatic example in the 1920s (and beyond) was the persistence of the identification of the presiding bishop with a particular diocese. The 1919 canon combined roles which might in theory seem to be mutually exclusive. The presiding bishop must be bishop of a diocese, and he would cease to be presiding bishop if he resigned his diocesan jurisdiction.[1] Yet his salary was to be paid by the General Convention; he was to be the executive head of the church's missionary, educational, and social work; and he was expected to reside at the national headquarters. This implicit tension was seen by some, at least, at the time. In 1924, one year before the first actual election of a presiding bishop, Dr. White saw the problem:[2]

> "The duties of the Presiding Bishop as executive head of all departments of the Church's work will require all his time, and he will be a Diocesan only in

name . . . The Presiding Bishop should be relieved of all Diocesan cares and responsibilities, and be able to give his whole time and thought to his larger duties as the executive head of the whole Church."

Yet it was not until 1943, almost twenty years later, that a canon both allowed and required a presiding bishop to resign his diocesan jurisdiction. For the next twenty years efforts were made to associate the presiding bishop with one particular diocese (usually Washington) or even to create a special, small diocese for him. Of the many committees and commissions which have considered this office in the twentieth century, the report of the Mutual Responsibility Commission in 1967 was the first *not* to recommend (or at least hope) that the office be identified with some particular diocese. The tradition that the presiding bishop would also be a diocesan bishop had enormous power and persistence, being officially abandoned by this church only in the late sixties and with obvious reluctance. So the old persists into the new.

That persistence may have been more than blind conservatism. As the inadequacy of the image of chief executive officer became apparent, thoughtful commentators looked to the past for insight and guidance as they explored a new and richer understanding of what a presiding bishop of this church might mean. Herein lies, I think, the reason for the apparently omnibus and shifting character of the role. Many General Conventions, including the one in Denver in 1979, were told that unrealistic expectations had been laid upon the occupant and that greater clarity of definition was needed. The last fifty years have certainly seen a far greater variety of understandings of that role than the previous century and a half. By 1919 it was clear that the older, classic view of that office would no longer suffice. But the new image embraced with such enthusiasm in 1919 of a chief executive soon itself began to be questioned. I think we can see the past sixty years as a sustained effort to explore new combinations and understandings, many of which did not break totally with the past. And it seems evident that the exploration is still continuing.

*　　　*　　　*

The constitution and canons were changed in 1919 to require a presiding bishop to be elected. But it was not until 1925 that the first election could take place. Bishop Tuttle was the venerable presiding bishop in 1919 and would remain so until his death. He died on April 17, 1923 in St. Louis, Missouri. Between that date and the next Convention in October, 1925 two senior bishops briefly held the office. Alexander Charles Garrett, Bishop of Dallas, succeeded as senior bishop in April, 1923. He was ninety-one years old and died eight months later at his home in Dallas. He in turn was succeeded by Ethelbert Talbot, Bishop of Bethlehem, who served for twenty-two months until the end of 1925 when the first elected presiding bishop took office. The brief term of the aged Bishop Garrett only brought home to some the wisdom of the change introduced in 1919. Frederick Cook Morehouse wrote in 1923 of the impossibility of a bishop who had not attended a General Convention since 1910 fulfilling the new duties:[3]

"None of the bishops has a stronger personality, none would have been a better advisor and guide . . . during the years of his youth . . . But that new and extensive duties should be laid upon anyone at so advanced an age, when nature itself suggests that the time for activity has passed, is a pathetic indication that the time for instituting an elective Presiding Bishopric was deferred much too long."

The General Convention of 1925 met in New Orleans. Before electing a presiding bishop, the House of Bishops received and adopted a thoughtful and searching report on the duties and the role of this new office.[4] A

Committee to Consider the Election of a Presiding Bishop carefully combed all the canons to draw together the many canonical duties of the presiding bishop: to preside at meetings of the House of Bishops, to take order for consecrations of bishops, to be especially responsible for missionary districts, to play a key role in the trial of bishops, to communicate with other Anglican provinces, etc. But the more interesting parts of the report were reflections on the nature of the office itself. The report noted that the presiding bishop was described in the new canon as the ". . . Executive and administrative head of the missionary, educational and social work of the Church," and they pointed out that this would mean new and increasing responsibilities beyond the specific ones mentioned by canons. For example, the report argued that he

". . . would appoint delegates to many Conferences and have to represent the Church in the Religious World upon many occasions and in connection with many movements. He is, to borrow the language of the state, the minister of Foreign Affairs."

But the committee was especially interested in his responsibilities within the church. They first spoke to some of the apprehensions about misuse of office:

"There is no hint of there being given to the Presiding Bishop, such as seems to be feared by some, any archiepiscopal powers, authorizing any interference in the internal affairs of a diocese."

One might observe in passing the rather curious idea that the distinctive characteristic of an archbishop was to interfere in the internal affairs of a diocese. But the most interesting part of this report was the understanding of chief executive officer:

"Your committee believes that an immense opportunity is opened to the Church to give and to follow a far-sighted unifying spiritual leadership. Administrative duties of the more technical and specialized kind may be largely devolved upon others, but thought for the whole Church, responsibility for the realizing of the Church's unity and guidance of the great policies of work should rest in the Presiding Bishop himself."

And at the end of their report, the Committee went even further:[5]

"However great the demand may be for administrative and executive capacity in the office, its supreme opportunity is spiritual. To interpret the Church's growing consciousness of her unity and of her mission to the world, to interpret it to both the Church and the world, to lead and inspire, to carry confidence and faith and develop devotion and loyalty, your Committee believes that such is the chief responsibility which will rest upon the Presiding Bishop."

That statement was, I believe, the finest and richest understanding of the new vision of the "Presiding Bishop of the Church" which any official body had yet produced. It is significant that the full report was adopted by the House of Bishops.

It can be argued that this view of the presiding bishop was simply a noble and high-level understanding of chief-executive-officer. Modern manuals on management usually emphasize the long-range and even visionary responsibilities of the chief executive. But the final terms of the committee's report, a call in 1925 for the presiding bishop to interpret, to lead and inspire, to carry confidence and faith, to develop devotion and loyalty does, I suggest, stretch the concept of chief executive considerably. Especially in the light of reports yet to come, we have here, I think, an early modification of the chief-executive-officer image and an early awareness that the 1919 actions had far deeper implications than simply executive and administrative ones. One does not usually say of a company president that his "supreme opportunity is spiritual."

For the first time in this church's history, the House of Bishops elected a presiding bishop in 1925. Although the deliberations were supposed to be secret, both candidates and ballots were widely reported. On the fourteenth ballot, John Gardner Murray, Bishop of Maryland, was elected presiding bishop. At his request, the Diocese of Maryland elected a coadjutor, and Murray took office on January 1, 1926. His term of office was to be a short one — he died during a meeting of the House of Bishops in October, 1929 — but even this short period made it clear that the new ideal would mean a very different presiding bishop. One of his earliest acts was to request each bishop to send him his photograph to hang in the Church Missions House. Many of the responses to Bishop Murray's request survive, and the bishops were obviously impressed and pleased at this new sense of personal unity being promoted by Bishop Murray. Furthermore, Bishop Murray announced his intention to travel — if possible to visit every diocese and missionary district. A testimony after his death noted that he "travelled thousands of miles in order to do this."

> "He traveled, not merely because he loved the opportunity to see the whole Church, but because he wanted the whole Church to understand that every Bishop's problems lay on his heart and every piece of work had his loving thought and prayer."

It was to be several years before the presiding bishop would be described a "chief pastor," but already that understanding of the office seems implicit in the ministry of John Gardner Murray.

*   *   *

Bishop Murray died on October 3, 1929. On November 13th the House of Bishops met in special session to elect a successor to fill the remainder of his term. As the election drew near, it became clear that the image of a chief executive officer was increasingly seen to be inadequate. The editor of *The Living Church* wrote:[7]

"Few realize how important the position has become . . . The Presiding Bishop is the chief executive of a business of some three to four million dollars a year. And he is a real executive . . . He has the same sort of responsibility that comes to every other head of a large business.

"And yet that is a particularly inadequate statement. He must not let the missionary venture become simply a phase of "Big Business." He is a spiritual force . . . In taking order for consecration of bishops, and in many other ways, he sustains an intimate relationship to every diocese. He is father in God to the whole Church. Bishop Murray created a position that is only simply outlined in the canons."

Once again, the election was fully reported although the meeting was in executive session. Charles Palmerston Anderson, Bishop of Chicago, was elected on the sixteenth ballot after a deadlock developed between the leading candidates.

Anderson was surprised; and although he accepted the election, he quickly announced that he would remain in Chicago and visit New York for special meetings. As he explained, "I have been elected . . . merely to fill a vacancy, a very short period of office . . . I do not want, at the end of two years, to find myself with nothing to do and no place to go. Therefore I cannot completely sever myself from the Diocese of Chicago, but I do intend to give a lot of time to the office."[8] It was a reasonable explanation, but an editorial in *The Living Church* showed just how strong the new image had become even during the short term of Bishop Murray. The editor feared that

". . . the governance of the Church by a bureaucracy

rather than primarily by a primate; a near reversion to the system that was ended, we hoped for all time, when the Presiding Bishopric was made an effective executive position. The chief value of Bishop Murray's primacy was in his daily contact with the workers in all departments of the Church's work."[9] But the whole issue came quickly to an end. Within a few weeks Bishop Anderson suffered a heart attack and died at his home on January 30, 1930.

*　　*　　*

The House of Bishops met in the midst of a Chicago blizzard on March 26, 1930 to elect a successor to finish Bishop Murray's term. This time there was no effort at secrecy, and on the seventh ballot James DeWolf Perry, Bishop of Rhode Island, was elected. When the General Convention met in September 1931 Perry was reelected to serve a regular six-year term.

Bishop Perry's correspondence has survived, and a brief sample provides a vivid picture of his day-to-day responsibilities. Here is the correspondence for a fairly light month, May of 1932.

May 6: He was concerned about a bishop who was feeble but reluctant to resign. Could an early pension be arranged for him?

May 7: He helped a returning missionary and his wife who had neither funds nor a home.

May 9: He appointed new members to the Commission on Christian Healing to replace those who had died.

May 9: He approved a shorter title for the Commission to Study the Disparity in Quotas and Budgets as Between Aided Dioceses and Missionary Districts.

May 9: He appointed the Rev. John W. Suter as the new custodian of the Book of Common Prayer.

May 16: He received an appeal from a missionary priest who complained about the actions of his bishop.

May 17: He received an appeal from a bishop about a private church task force that was in his diocese.

May 19: He answered a confidential letter describing allegedly factional and racist actions in a diocesan election. Perry expressed his "earnest sympathy" and concluded: "Fortunately the church has wonderful powers of restabilization. God does use our human efforts, however feeble and blundering they may be, that his will may be done. The best we can do is to adjust our thought and action to these utilimate purposes and to trust that the utterances and decisions of individuals or conventions may be used in the end for his glory."

May 19: He consulted with another bishop about a committee agenda.

May 20: He commended a prominent clergyman for a courageous and healing witness which he had made at a recent diocesan convention.

May 24: He responded to a protest at which non-episcopally ordained clergymen participated in a service of Holy Communion.

May 25: He agreed to endorse an effort to raise a memorial fund for a prominent Scottish bishop.

May 27: He issued the judgment that twenty-three fine copies of the 1892 Prayer Book should be kept and not given away.

May 31: He welcomed a committee of the House of Bishops who were to consult with the National Council staff about the current financial crisis.

May 31: He confirmed the jurisdiction of a bishop in a newly divided diocese and appointed another bishop to preside at the service of installation.

Bishop Perry's correspondence for a light but typical month conveys the overwhelming impression of a significant leader who was involved in and consulted by a large number of different people in this church. Often he was called upon to give care and thoughtful counsel in difficult personal and private situations involving either priests or bishops. The dominant tone of his letters was his compassionate concern both for individuals and for the well-being of the church.[10]

Bishop Perry was halfway through his six-year term when the General Convention met in Atlantic City in 1934. It had not been easy for Perry to combine his duties as diocesan of Rhode Island with the expanded expectations of an elected presiding bishop. He secured the assistance of a retired bishop to help in Rhode Island, and his journal shows that he spent about half his time in New York. But the combination was a heavy one.[11] The Convention made some effort to ease the burden by electing the Right Rev. Philip Cook, Bishop of Delaware, as President of the National Council with the hope that he could share some of the administrative burden. By 1935 Perry was able to move permanently back to Rhode Island, but the compromise was soon seen to be a poor one.[12]

More signficant were two proposals in 1934 affecting the office. As we have seen, the Convention expected even an elected presiding bishop to retain a diocesan jurisdiction. Now, for the first time, General Convention approached the idea of a permanent see for that elected person. The Bishop of Albany moved that ". . . in view of the somewhat widely expressed opinion that the residence of the Presiding Bishop should be at the Capital of the Nation" the Diocese of Washington be asked if they would give the matter "sympathetic consideration." The resolution was easily adopted by both houses.[13] In the 1960s the idea of a permanent see for the presiding bishop was to be dismissed as romantic and sentimental. Perhaps it was by then, but it was not so thirty years earlier. A correspondent to *The Churchman* used colorful and angry language to express his dissatisfaction with the new arrangement. The presiding bishop was, he wrote,

". . . a bishop amputated from his diocese, suspended, as it were, in *vacuo,* with only 281 for

81

cathedra and see. Like a tree without roots, like a stream without a source, a joke without a point, he presides over bishops . . . and wanders vaguely about the land, primatial but unprecedented."[14]

A calmer and more reasoned statement of the problem was offered by Bishop Perry himself in a stirring address to the House of Bishops in 1937, as his term was coming to an end.

"You mechanize the Presiding Bishop when you tie him to a desk simply as an administrator . . . When you speak of removing a Presiding Bishop from his physical presence in his own diocese, to *what* are you removing him? To a desk in an office building, four floors up. You are asking him to leave the exercise of his priesthood . . . you are moving him into the jurisdiction of another bishop."

And he challenged "the one hundred potential Presiding Bishops in the House." How would you ". . . adapt yourselves to the fact of being constantly in a diocese where another bishop has jurisdiction?." Perry sat down to "tumultuous applause."[15]

The presiding bishop had stated the problem clearly and personally. For some years Convention toyed with the idea of a particular see — perhaps Washington, perhaps a token creation — as a solution. Eventually that solution was unacceptable, but the problem remains to this day.

Even more striking was the proposal in 1934 to change the canon on the duties of the presiding bishop. The House of Deputies received a report from the Committee on the Status and Work of the Presiding Bishop and actually passed a new section of Canon 17. The canon repeated the traditional duties of president of the House of Bishops and chief consecrator of bishops. Then three new sections were added.[16]

"He shall be official representative of the Church in all communications and dealings with other

Churches, religious bodies and organizations throughout the world.

"He shall be Chief Pastor of the Church, with the duty to plan for its future growth and work in the advancement of the Kingdom of God.

"He shall visit all parts of the country, bringing to every section a sense of the Church's solidarity, and shall speak for the Church to the great multitudes of the unchurched."

The bishops did not concur with this change, and it did not find its way into the canons. But if the report of 1925 stretched the concept of chief executive officer to the limit, the proposed canon of 1934 would have replaced it altogether. The images that stand out here are "representative," "visitor," "speaker for the Church," and above all, "Chief Pastor."

*　　　*　　　*

As the General Convention of 1937 approached, it was clear that the compromise of 1934 was not working well. A bishop of Rhode Island who was presiding bishop and a bishop of Delaware who was President of the National Council hardly provided the kind of energetic central leadership envisaged since 1919. On October 4th and 5th the National Council held a full and lengthy discussion. All the issues emerged once again, but the main concern of the Council was the need for a truly full-time presiding bishop. Bishop Cook, President of the National Council, summarized the discussion:[17]

"Unless we can get the full time of the Presiding Bishop, our work will suffer. We *must* have his full time. When we begin the question of the title of the Presiding Bishop or the question of primatial jurisdiction, we are bringing to the question matters for which the Church is not prepared. But the Church *is* ready to vote on the status of the Presiding Bishop, but *not yet* on his title nor the locus of his jurisdiction. Let us not confuse the issue."

Their solution was to propose that the presiding bishop continue officially as a diocesan bishop (lest he lose his right to a seat at the Lambeth Conference), but that a diocese be required to elect a coadjutor for the actual work of the diocese. They further proposed that the elected presiding bishop serve until he was seventy, during which service he would be resident in New York and fully occupied as presiding bishop.

Others besides the National Council were also concerned. The Joint Committee on the Status and Work of the Presiding Bishop presented an extended report, as thoughtful and even more far-reaching than the report of 1925.[18] This report began by acknowledging that present arrangements were "not working well" and that ". . . our experience thus far has compelled us to face the fact that we have no right to ask any man to carry this double burden" of being both a diocesan and a presiding bishop.

It is noteworthy that the committee found only two possible solutions: election of a bishop coadjutor ". . . to whom the Presiding Bishop should be required to delegate a jurisdiction which would relieve him of all but nominal duties in his diocese" or the "creation of a See for the Presiding Bishop." So strong was the tradition that the presiding bishop *must* be identified with a particular diocese that the solution eventually adopted in 1943, which simply required the presiding bishop to resign his diocesan jurisdiction, did not even occur as a serious possibility in the report of 1937. The committee chose the first solution and expressed the hope that the second might develop, especially through "a concordat with the Diocese of Washington."

The report concluded with two thoughtful paragraphs on titles and on the symbolism of the office. Throughout the statement on titles run familiar themes about an American church.

"It will be noted that the Committee has not concerned itself about nor recommended any change in the title of the office. . . . The title Presiding Bishop has been consecrated for us by the men who have held it. It is part of our national Church life and experience. Moreover, the Presiding Bishop, by virtue of the duties which he now performs, is Primate and Metropolitan whatever title he holds. It might be worth our while to pass a resolution in General Convention that whatever title is printed in official documents these words, 'Primate and Metropolitan,' should follow such title, but we make no recommendation."

Even more significant was the committee's understanding of the symbolic meaning of the office:[19]

"We would say that this Church needs, increasingly, a visible symbol of its national unity. Provinces may in the future be given additional powers by General Convention. We may seek to develop a more intelligent policy of Church extension by paying more heed to local needs . . . But we shall need all the more a growing sense of our national reponsibility for the work as a whole. No committee like the National Council, nor any large assemblage like the General Convention — representative in a way as they are — can ever be as truly symbolic as an individual leader. This accords with the facts of human nature and with the central truth of the Christian Religion — the Incarnation of the Son of God."

The presiding bishop was to be a symbol of the unity of the Church — and the Incarnation itself was invoked as authority!

The Convention of 1937 spent some time considering various aspects of the office. It was clear that neither the executive efficiency nor the ideal of chief executive officer embraced with such enthusiasm in 1919 had come to pass. After much debate, the Convention took two significant actions. Canon 17 was amended to require the presiding bishop ". . . to relinquish the administration of his Diocese sufficiently to enable him fully to perform his duties as Presiding Bishop." And the same canon abolished the six-year term in favor of an indefinite term with retirement at the age of sixty-eight.[20] At the same time Convention invited the presiding bishop to deliver an opening sermon which would go far beyond his report of official acts and be based upon his knowledge of "the needs and work of the whole church."[21]

But the basic question of the nature of the office itself would not go away. The possibility of a permanent see in Washington was again discussed. The Diocese of Washington reported that it was officially ". . . entirely sympathetic with the resolution of the General Convention in 1934 looking to the residence of the Presiding Bishop in Washington;" but in fact Bishop Freeman of Washington was strongly opposed to that diocese relinquishing its right to elect its own bishop,[22] and the idea was simply referred again to committee. A layman from the Diocese of Quincy proposed that the presiding bishop "be given the official title of Primate" but the motion lost in the House of Deputies.[23]

More significant were resolutions which tried to embody some of the language and ideals of the Joint Committee on the Status and Work of the Presiding Bishop. On October 11th, the House of Bishops considered and approved a resolution which would have gone far to redefine the nature of the office. That resolution declared that

". . . the office and work of the Presiding Bishop is first and foremost one of spiritual leadership, and second, that of shared responsibility for the government and administration of the Church's temporal concerns.

"As a spiritual leader, the Presiding Bishop is a

witness-in-chief to Christ, missionary of missionaries, first in every forward movement, and Father-in-God to the Bishops. Through him, under proper provision, *the Church may make known to the World the Gospel of Christ in application to the problems of the age.*"

The Deputies were willing to accept that resolution provided that a caution be added:

"Except as may therein be provided it is not intended to abridge any of the powers and rights heretofore and now lawfully belonging to any Bishop and to every other member of this Church on questions of Doctrine, Faith and Worship, and the application of the Gospel of Christ to the problems of the age."

The House of Bishops did not like this caution and the entire matter was dropped.[24]

Although the canons adopted in 1937 did not imply any fundamental change in the conception of the office, it is clear that some basic thinking about that position was going on. The report of the Joint Committee, the resolution adopted by the Bishops, as well as the canon adopted only by the deputies in 1934 are all based on very significant modifications of the image of "chief executive officer." "Chief pastor" and "official representative" were key terms in the 1934 proposal. Now a new and significant note is sounded: the presiding bishop is to have a prophetic role — he is to be "witness-in-chief to Christ" and to "make known to the World the Gospel of Christ in application to the problems of the age." That note was not officially approved in 1937, but it was to recur again and again.

*　　　*　　　*

On balance there was general satisfaction with the results of the Cincinnati Convention. Henry St. George

Tucker, Bishop of Virginia since 1927, was elected the new presiding bishop on the second ballot. Bishop Tucker had served in Japan from 1899 until 1923, having been consecrated Bishop of Kyoto in 1912. A leading editorial in *The Living Church* concluded that

"Bishop Tucker's primacy will inaugurate a new era of missionary advance ... The new Presiding Bishop ... will have greatly increased power in the administration of the Church's missionary affairs ...[and] a new place of leadership in the formation of the policies of the Church.[25]"

Howard Chandler Robbins, in a sermon at St. Bartholomew's Church, New York City, also saw considerable significance in the 1937 actions:[26]

"... the definition of the work and status of the Presiding Bishop has been made in what may be called missionary terms. His term of office no longer a six-year term but a life work, limited only by age; the conferring of greater executive powers upon him than have heretofore been centered in any single person; the requirement of him not only of all the time that he can spare from his diocesan obligations but of all the time that he requires; and the selection of our next Presiding Bishop of one who has actually spent many many years in missionary service and who from personal experience is acquainted with the needs of the mission fields; These things ... entitle the General Convention of 1937 to the honorable name of a missionary convention."

In accordance with both the spirit and the intent of Canon 17, Bishop Tucker announced to his diocese that he would almost exclusively devote his time to the work of the presiding bishop. Yet the *Journal* of that diocese show that his close ties to Virginia continued to be significant. He attended every diocesan convention until 1943 (when he finally resigned); his comments, his annual addresses (usually delivered without notes), and the frequent references to his presence are signs of the reality of the ties that remained.

Virginia already had a coadjutor bishop in 1937, the Right Rev. Frederick D. Goodwin. In 1938 Bishop Goodwin told the diocese in his annual address that,

> "Bishop Tucker is fitted as we believe no other man in the Church is fitted to give inspiration and leadership in his difficult task. At the end of [his term] . . . we will welcome him back as the actual as well as the titular head of the Diocese. Meanwhile . . . whatever adjustments may be necessary . . . will be gladly made, and we will count them as Virginia has always counted her contribution to the missionary cause, a privilege."[27]

The changes in 1937 envisaged a much more streamlined and efficient central office, and Tucker carried out that mandate with tact and diplomacy. His colleague and friend, Charles W. Sherrin, wrote:[28]

> "Beginning with the selection and appointment of missionaries, through the many details of material arrangements, great advancement in more efficient work has been made. . . The procedure was difficult, for personalities were involved. Some men had to be demoted; some had to be dismissed; and it took a spiritual giant to accomplish such things with a minimum of hurt feelings."

In 1940 the General Convention met in Kansas City, Missouri amid the deepening shadows of world-wide war. In a letter read to the open House of Bishops, the Archbishop of Canterbury reported that "a German bomb last week destroyed a considerable part of Lambeth and I shall be unable to live there during the war, perhaps never again."[29] Bishop Tucker called upon the church both before and during Convention to a Forward in Service movement "on the whole front of the Church's life and work," and the Convention responded with enthusiasm. Charles W. Sheerin wrote, "In all fairness I don't believe any one can call Bishop Tucker a great orator, but that day we felt the inspiration that must have been given him by God, for never in my lifetime, have I seen people so moved."[30] A joint session passed a resolution expressing the hope ". . . that the two Houses of the Convention will take appropriate action requesting the Presiding Bishop to carry on this Forward Movement under his wise and inspiring personal leadership."[31]

In general the new arrangement adopted in 1937 seemed to be working fairly well. The major issue was the unsatisfactory arrangement of a presiding bishop who was still a diocesan bishop. As the Joint Commission to Consider the Matter of a See for the Presiding Bishop put it in their report, "It is most desirable that he should not retain jurisdiction in his previous Diocese, which might be thousands of miles from National Headquarters." The Commission proposed that the ". . . Cathedral in Washington, D.C., be and hereby is designated as the Seat of the Presiding Bishop for his use on occasions incident to the exercise of his office as Presiding Bishop" and they went on to point out that the new arrangement did not alter the legal status of the cathedral, its bishop or dean.

"The situation necessitates a seat in, rather than jurisdiction over said Cathedral. Our recommendations leave the present legal status of the Cathedral Foundation undisturbed, with the Bishop of Washington as head of such Foundation."

In making this recommendation the commission was careful to reject any implication that this action would imply an archiepiscopal character for the office. In fact, the commission returned to chief executive officer images to underscore their caution. He has, they wrote,

". . . general oversight of the Missionary Districts; and is Executive Head of the National Council . . .

"The office of the Presiding Bishop differs definitely from that of the traditional archbishop in that he has no jurisdiction over other Bishops in matters of faith and order. His duties are more arduous, and his power less hierarchical than those of an Archbishop in the Church of England."[32]

The recommendations of the Joint Commission were approved by both Houses without division.

Accordingly Bishop Tucker was installed in the National Cathedral on October 24, 1941. He is reported to have commented that now, like all Gaul, he "was divided into three parts." "Y'all know," he said, "that my heart is in Virginia, and my headquarters are in New York, and now they tell me that my seat is in Washington!"[33]

The Joint Commission was prepared to let the matter rest there, but the Convention as a whole was not yet satisfied. A seat was one thing; bishop of a diocese was a different one. Accordingly, the Convention adopted on first reading an amendment to the constitution which would allow General Convention ". . . to establish a See for the Presiding Bishop which may embrace the whole or part of a Diocese now existing or hereafter formed."[34] That amendment was to die in Convention in 1943, but the concern that the presiding bishop be bishop of *a* diocese has been a very deep one in this Church.

Bishop Tucker continued to preside at the conventions of the Diocese of Virginia after 1940. He contributed to a discussion about the World War at the Convention of 1941, called for a suffragan to assist Bishop Goodwin in 1942, and reported to the Convention of 1943 that he had also been elected President of the Federal Council of Churches. Bishop Goodwin, the coadjutor bishop, told the convention of Virginia that he and the new suffragan would try to relieve Bishop Tucker ". . . as far as he will permit us, of diocesan responsibilities that he may be free as possible for the larger duties which he alone as Presiding Bishop and President of the Federal Council can fulfill."[35] But one certainly gains the impression from the records of that Convention that Bishop Tucker's ties to Virginia were far from nominal or insignificant.

*   *   *

The General Convention of 1940 had requested Bishop Tucker to open the next Convention with a sermon, and he did so with another long and stirring call for expanded missionary work at home and abroad, which he called "Forward in Service," for service to a post-war world, for support of the Presiding Bishop's Fund for World Relief, and for renewed commitment to the Christ who is the source of all mission.

"If we are to become God's agents in saving the world of our generation from either spiritual or physical peril, we must be animated by a like love. Such love cannot be humanly generated. It is the gift of God, manifested and made available by the Cross of Christ and shed abroad in our hearts by the Holy Spirit."[36]

Even today, the power and force of that address come through the yellowed pages of *The Living Church*'s reprint. The address is as striking for what it omits as for what it includes. The House of Bishops who had elected Henry St. George Tucker in 1937 had defined the office of Presiding Bishop in part as ". . . a witness-in-chief to Christ, missionary of missionaries, first in every forward movement, and Father-in-God to the Bishops." Bishop Tucker's opening address in 1943 could not have been more faithful to that mandate. But the bishops had also gone on to add: "Through him . . . the Church may make known to the World the Gospel of Christ in application to the problems of the age." The presiding bishop's address was less faithful to that part of the bishops' mandate. The great issues of war and peace, of justice and freedom, of human rights remained untouched. The kind of concerns which the Federal Council of Churches expressed in their well-known document, "A Just and

Durable Peace" (more popularly known by its shortened form, "The Six Pillars of Peace") issued on December 11, 1942 were outside the scope of Bishop Tucker's address.[37] My point is not that Bishop Tucker was uninterested in questions of peace and justice. He became president of the Federal Council of Churches in 1942 and continued to support the Council's statement on peace. Rather, at his great address before the convention in 1943, Tucker clearly saw his role as that of chief missionary, "missionary of missionaries;" and he summoned the church with a striking call to mission. This image, rather than that of social prophet, was the one conveyed to the huge opening service at the Cleveland General Convention of 1943.

That Convention took only two significant actions in regard to the presiding bishop. The first was to continue Bishop Tucker in office! Canon 17, as amended in 1937, required the presiding bishop to retire at the Convention following his sixty-eighth birthday. Tucker was sixty-nine in 1943 and canonically due to retire. However 1943 was not a time when change was desired (the larger issue of the Presbyterian-Episcopal concordat was neatly postponed also in 1943), and Convention allowed Tucker to continue by the simple expedient of amending the canon to require retirement at seventy. (The age was returned to sixty-eight in 1946.)

The other action was to make the final break with the old tradition of a presiding bishop who was also bishop of a diocese. By now, the enormous difficulty of that double burden was clear, and the arrangements with Washington seemed to offer a reasonable sense of an ecclesiastical locus. That a break would come was inevitable. The reasons given by the Joint Committee to Consider the Matter of a See for the Presiding Bishop are especially interesting. One issue was the question raised in 1937 of the presiding bishop's right to attend Lambeth Conferences if he did not have a diocesan jurisdiction. The Commission on Policy and Strategy actually requested a

93

ruling from England and received a "personal opinion" from Archbishop William Temple that

> ". . . if the Church in America were to decide that the duties of that office were so exacting that the occupant of that office ought not to have any Diocese, we should certainly regard his position as itself constituting a jurisdiction, and that the Presiding Bishop would not forfeit his place in the Lambeth Conference if he had no Diocese."[18]

A second issue was the question of jurisdiction. The joint committee argued that in fact ". . . the Presiding Bishop already has a jurisdiction which though not territorial is real and defined by Canon" and they pointed to his presidency of the National Council, his oversight of missionary districts and the American Churches in Europe, as well as his responsibilities for the consecration of all bishops. They did *not* say (as has sometimes been implied by commentators) that he has jurisdiction over the entire American church.[39]

But even if the break were to be made, the bishops at least were willing to see it only as an interim step. The bishops were given an *ad interim* report which emphasized the importance of the honorary position the presiding bishop now had in Washington. The committee hoped that report

> ". . . may lead naturally and by common consent to a further development, looking toward the future establishment of a separate and independent See or Jurisdiction for the Presiding Bishop and the building in Washington of a suitable Residence for the Presiding Bishop, and the establishment there of the spiritual centre of the work of the Episcopal Church in the United States."[40]

The change in canon was to come, but along with that change the Joint Committee was charged to continue its work since it was ". . . desirable that a See be provided in which the Presiding Bishop may exercise jurisdiction and perform the function of his Office as a Bishop."[41]

It was with many misgivings then that the canon on the presiding bishop was amended to read:[42]

"Upon the expiration of the term of office of the Presiding Bishop, the Bishop who is elected to succeed him shall tender to the House of Bishops his resignation of his previous jurisdiction, to take effect upon the date of his assuming the office of Presiding Bishop, or not later than six (6) months thereafter."

Although the canon technically exempted Tucker, he followed its spirit and announced his resignation as Bishop of Virginia. The *Journals* of that diocese make it clear that Tucker's resignation was much more than a *pro forma* matter. The Diocesan Convention of 1944 was a moving one. A testimonial dinner for Tucker brought many expressions of love and affection. Bishop Goodwin, his successor, told the diocese:

"I know Virginia is proud that he continues as Presiding Bishop. No other call would have taken him even temporarily from his Diocese . . . We look forward to his return to his native soil when his duties as Presiding Bishop are fulfilled; and our word to him now and tonight is not goodbye but 'Well done, keep it up, and come back home when you can.' "[43]

In 1945, for the first time in eighteen years, Bishop Tucker was not present at the Convention of Virginia, although the editors of the *Journal* for that year printed a full-page photograph of their former bishop.

*   *   *

Thus came quietly to an end one of the oldest traditions associated with the office of presiding bishop. But even in 1943 the matter did not quite end. The Joint Commission to Consider a See continued its work and in 1946 presented a report which actually called for the creation of a new small diocese out of the County of Arlington, Virginia. The new diocese would have four self-supporting parishes and just over 1100 communicants. The reasons the committee gave were the most interesting part of an extended report (which included a map of the proposed diocese).

"We are profoundly convinced that the present situation in which the Presiding Bishop has no territorial jurisdiction is one that is anomalous and contrary to the age-long and unbroken custom of the Church, necessitating as it does that our Presiding Bishop, in order to perform any of his Episcopal offices as a Bishop of the Church of God, is obliged to do so by courtesy only of some other Bishop or of some parish priest."

And they added that they did not think the present arrangements were ". . . consonant with the dignity of the office of the Presiding Bishop of this Church, or with the inherent rights, privileges and duties of a Bishop in the Church."[44]

But this proposal ran headlong into the plans of the new presiding bishop, Henry Knox Sherrill. "Henry Knox Sherrill, D.D., LL.D., Bishop of Massachusetts, was found on the first ballot to have received a canonical majority of votes and was thereupon declared by the Chair to have been chosen the Presiding Bishop of this Church."[45] He was the first presiding bishop in the history of this church who was required to resign his jurisdiction upon becoming presiding bishop. The next day the Joint Committee to Consider a See presented its report, but its motion to establish a "territorial See for the Presiding Bishop" was rejected and the committee itself discharged.[46]

The Living Church commented dryly:[47]

"The House of Bishops gave the *coup de grace,* early in its sessions, for the proposal for a Primatial See of

96

Arlington. One of the bishops commented that the Presiding Bishop was already buried in the grave of "281", and it would only make matters worse to inter him in the national cemetary of Arlington. Some day, perhaps, the Church will have a proper and dignified ecclesiastical home for its chief bishop, rather than merely a business office."

Bishop Sherrill indeed did want a permanent residence, but not in Washington. He urged the General Convention to provide

". . . in the vicinity of New York a suitable residence for the Presiding Bishop, a Chapel, an Hostel for the entertainment of Bishops and Missionaries who may from time to time find it necessary to consult with the Presiding Bishop and National Council, and perhaps a suitable dwelling for certain permanent members of the National Council."

The Convention agreed and in 1947 the Satterlee estate near Greenwich, Connecticut was acquired. Bishop Sherrill reported that he was tempted to name the new house in honor of Bishop William White but then decided that "Seabury House" would be preferable to "White House."

One other minor but significant action was taken in 1946, namely to provide an official seal for the presiding bishop. In a letter to the chairman of the Joint Commission on Church Architecture, Bishop Tucker explained the problem he faced in 1943:

"Up to the present, the Presiding Bishop has been also Bishop of a Diocese, and in attaching a seal to official documents naturally used the seal of his Diocese. Now, however, he is required to relinquish his Diocese, and I am wondering whether it would not be a good thing to have a seal for the Presiding Bishop.

"Of course, nothing official could be adopted, I suppose, except by action of General Convention; but if in the meanwhile some one who is expert in these matters could give me the design for a suggested seal I could use it temporarily, instead of signing official documents with a ten cent piece, as I have sometimes had to do."

A seal was proposed by the Commission and adopted by the Convention.[48] Evidently prior to 1946 Bishop Tucker also used it as his personal seal instead of a ten cent piece.

Henry Knox Sherrill was presiding bishop for almost twelve years, from January 1, 1947 to November 14, 1958. Since 1919 almost continuous debate and legislation had come before every General Convention about that office, but by 1946 a workable compromise seemed to be at hand. During Sherrill's twelve-year term, issues and questions relating to the office were conspicuous by their absence from the *Journals* of General Convention.

Bishop Sherrill brought to the office a rich background of service as rector of the Church of Our Saviour, Brookline, Massachusetts, then rector of Trinity Church, Boston, and finally as Bishop of Massachusetts. It is not possible to do more than suggest the richness of life and service which Sherrill gave to this church. His own autobiography, *Among Friends,* reveals a full and varied ministry. Of many stories, I report only one which was typical of the way Henry Knox Sherrill carried out his ministry. Here is his account of his first meeting with the vestry of Trinity Church.[49]

"Our first meeting was held in Mr. Hutchins's law office . . . and very soon it became clear that we were facing a critical situation in regard to the support asked of Trinity for the work of our church at home and abroad. In the current year it appeared that we were almost $30,000 behind our pledge, which came as a shock to me. Mr. Hutchins announced this fact and then added, 'We have decided to let this year go and to concentrate our energies on reaching the full amount next year. Dr. Mann left in January, and our new Rector has come in May. This deficit, therefore, is the responsibility of neither.'

"I spoke up almost immediately. 'It is not a matter of whose responsibility this is, whether Dr. Mann's or mine. The question is what happens to the salaries of the missionaries in the field.'

"Mr. Hutchins said, 'This has been decided.'

"To which I replied, 'This has not been decided so far as I am concerned. The parish has a right to know the facts. Next Sunday I propose to appeal to the congregation, if necessary, over the heads of the wardens and vestry.'

"There were a few moments of silence. Then Mr. Hutchins reached in his pocket, took out a piece of paper, wrote on it, passed it by me to Mr. Paine, and so it was handed on to the members of the vestry. I had no idea what this meant and the thought passed through my mind that they were being polled on my resignation.

"When the paper was returned to Mr. Hutchins, he announced, 'We have just subscribed so-many thousand dollars toward the needed amount. Gentlemen, there is a balance in the Treasury. I would like to have a motion that this too be added.' It was carried. Then Mr. Hutchins, in his courtly manner, bowed to me and concluded: 'Mr. Rector, we hope that next Sunday you will ask the congregation for the balance to make up the full amount with the entire support of the wardens and vestry.'

"I have always felt that the future of my leadership of the parish hung in the balance of those first minutes of my initial meeting. The next Sunday I asked for the full amount and the money was given. We were on our way."

This typical incident reveals much about the ministry of Henry Knox Sherrill. He was at home in the presence of influential and wealthy people; he was effective in raising funds for the work of the church; and he was uncompromising in his support for the missionary work of the church. His son, the Rev. Franklin Goldwaite Sherrill, reported that above all else, Bishop Sherrill thought of himself as "chief missionary." Presidency of the Domestic and Foreign Missionary Society was integral to his work as presiding bishop. He sponsored the Builders for Christ program, a revolving loan fund which enabled the building of several hundred churches and eventually developed into the Episcopal Church Foundation. He maintained close personal contact especially with missionary bishops through letters and visits. He was concerned about ecumenical issues and supported the Presbyterian-Episcopal concordat of 1946. Questions of social ethics, especially those relating to medical developments, concerned him also. He was a person with deep friendships, a strong family life, and a rich sense of humor.

Although no person ever fits completely within one image, my impression is that he came closest to fulfilling the idea set forth in 1919 and 1925 as a chief executive officer who is primarily concerned for the mission of this church and its vigorous prosecution. He was devoted to Bishop Tucker (and in fact, worked for Tucker's election in 1937). Like Tucker, he was a ". . . witness-in-chief to Christ, missionary of missionaries, first in every forward movement, and Father-in-God to the Bishops."[50]

Near the end of his term, he began to touch upon a new theme which would be even more prominent in the addresses of his successor, namely the unity of sacred and secular issues. In his opening address to the Convention of 1955, he said:[51]

"I can dream of a Church which realizes that God works through every agency of life. There can never, therefore, be any sharp delineation between the spiritual and the secular . . . Are we to leave the moral issues of nuclear warfare to groups of scientists? or the spiritual implications of the race problem to the courts? . . . No, the Church with an humble realization of the complexity of modern problems nevertheless has a responsibility to state great ethical and spiritual principles."

The Living Church, which often disagreed with Sherrill, aptly described him as "a symbol of efficiency as well as of spiritual leadership." In 1962 he concluded a remarkable vigorous autobiography with this moving paragraph:[52]

"As I anticipate the inevitability of death, it is not without some personal questions. God's ways are not our ways and He has reason for judgment of us all. But in the light of Christ's message of forgiveness and of love, in the hope of the Cross and of the Resurrection, in the fellowship of loved ones who have gone on before, without attempting to imagine any details or circumstances, I look forward to the life of the world to come."

*　　*　　*

The General Convention of 1958 faced the task of electing a successor to Bishop Sherrill. It would, of course, be unrealistic not to recognize that a small but significant number of church people were unhappy about Sherrill's administration. One prominent priest in Atlanta wrote a typical letter to *The Living Church.*[53]

"The church is being taken out of the hands of its members, and being made the property of a small, clever, liberal clique who try to impose their partisan policies on everyone, and regard as disloyal anyone who won't agree with them."

Bishop Sherrill's own opening sermon at the 1958 Convention spoke directly to that charge. In fact, by 1958 far more significant voices than the angry priest from Atlanta had some misgivings about the office. *The Living Church* returned to the old theme of a presiding bishop without a diocese. We need a presiding bishop, the editor wrote, who is less administrative and more episcopal. And that journal urged the creation of a small see, perhaps in western Connecticut, which would ". . . not only allow the Presiding Bishop to function as a bishop but also would allow him the time and peace in which to meet the pressing and heavy duties that inevitably fall to him as the spiritual leader, spokesman, and chief strategist of the Church."[54]

Reservations were also expressed at the Convention itself. A proposal was presented to reactivate the old Joint Committee on the Office and Work of the Presiding Bishop because ". . . we have obviously allowed the duties of the Presiding Bishop to be increased to the danger point because of our failure to define our own aims for the nature of this office, expecting in one man to find our Spiritual leadership as well as the business administrator." However the Joint Committee on Committees and Commissions recommended nonconcurrance because ". . . the Committee believes that it would be wiser to refrain from establishing such a commission during the early period of the term of a new Presiding Bishop."[55]

In any case, the Convention did elect a very different person to be the next presiding bishop. Arthur Lichtenberger, born in Wisconsin, then Bishop of Missouri, was elected on the third ballot. He had served in China, Cincinnati, Brookline, Newark, and the General Theological Seminary before becoming bishop coadjutor of Missouri in 1950 and diocesan in 1952.

Something of the different approach which Arthur Lichtenberger brought to the office can be seen by comparing Bishop Sherrill's final charge to the Convention of 1958 with Bishop Lichtenberger's installation sermon of 1959 and his first charge to the General Convention of 1961. In 1958 Sherrill urged support for the Church of South India, reorganization of the

102

structure of General Convention, support for the budget of the National Council, the value of Lambeth Conferences, the importance of "personal confrontation of the individual with the living God" and a call to loyalty to Christ.[56]

Lichtenberger, at his installation a few months later, emphasized two themes: mission and unity. But mission now had a broader and more sweeping character.

"There is only one place at which a genuine renewal of the life of the Church can take place, namely at the point at which its mission of transforming the world is being fulfilled. The only real renewal is a healing and saving manifestation of the power of love in open and courageous encounter with the world."

And again:[57]

"The gospel speaks to the totality of life; all that we do individually or together, stands under the judgment of God."

In 1961 Lichtenberger called the church to conversion from the world and to God: to the humility to recognize that God is at work everywhere;

". . . in the researches of the scientists . . . in the deliberations of the United Nations . . . in the course of events in Berlin and Havana . . ."

and not just in the church; to obedience in mission which could mean a reconciling role in the midst of racial conflict and a fresh commitment to the unity of the church.[58]

There was widespread satisfaction with the grace and charm which Lichtenberger brought to the office. In 1961 *The Living Church* noted that, "Bishop Lichtenberger, as Presiding Bishop, has won the confidence of all schools of thought in the Church as one who is not only fair but loving, not only intelligent but wise;" and a reporter earlier had described the meetings of the National Council as proceeding with ". . . a minimum of debate and confusion and with continuous good humor and unflustered dispatch. The sessions have been businesslike but relaxed in atmosphere."[59]

But the question of a see for the presiding bishop would not go away. Shortly before the 1961 Convention, the distinguished Bishop of Rhode Island, John S. Higgins, returned to the matter in an article:[60]

"Does not our Church need an archbishop with the appropriate jurisdiction that goes historically with the office? And would it not be better for such a chief pastor to have his headquarters at a cathedral rather than in an office building? Since we have determined to build a new headquarters office in midtown New York, it is my hope that we shall one day dispose of it at a handsome profit, and arrange for the headquarters of our national Church to be at the national cathedral in the national capital where it properly belongs, and from which the life of our Episcopal Church should radiate."

The significance of these many references to an association with Washington is clear, I think, if we recall this church's understanding of its symbolic identity as that identity developed in the late nineteenth century. The idea of a national church, now transformed into the bridge church,[61] was still alive and vigorous. If this was to be a national church, playing a unique role as a bridge church between protestantism and catholicism, then where better should its national center be than the capital of the nation.

The note which stands out more clearly than any other as a new one in Arthur Lichtenberger's term is a prophetic one; more than any previous presiding bishop, he was concerned with relating the gospel to the great issues of justice and freedom which were beginning to dominate this country's internal life. That note was already implicit in his installation address and it became increasingly clear in the next few years. In an undated sermon, probably from around 1962, he wrote,

"The Church is to be concerned with all that affects man's life in the world, with economics and politics and public morality. Those . . . who in the name of the gospel and patriotism tell us that the Church must not speak out on such public issues, do not, I submit, understand the gospel or know the meaning of true patriotism."

Or again:

"The revolutionary changes of our time are not a mistake; they are not taking place without God."

In 1963 he called upon the church for specific actions to eliminate racial discrimination within its life.[62]

"it is not enough for the Church to exhort men to be good . . . Discrimination within the Body of the Church itself is an intolerable scandal. Every congregation has a continuing need to examine its own life and to renew those efforts necessary to insure its inclusiveness fully."

And in his last book, *The Day is at Hand* (1964), he wrote of "The Church Called to Act in Public Affairs:"[63]

"The struggle for racial justice is of the utmost importance and gravity for us in this country . . . We are called to repentance for the way we have accepted and perpetuated racial divisions, repentance for the unloving and unwise ways in which we have attempted to break down those divisions, and repentance for our indifference and blindness. And we are called to obedience in asking God to show us his way, and in seeking to be makers of his peace."

As we have seen, a report to the General Convention in 1937 called upon the presiding bishop to be a voice by which ". . . the Church may make known to the World the Gospel of Christ in application to the problems of the age."[64] That concern was, of course, not absent from the ministry of earlier men, but it stands out more clearly and singly in the presidency of Arthur Lichtenberger than in any of his predecessors.

One of the sad developments in the years before the 1964 General Convention was the progressive illness of Arthur Lichtenberger. Parkinson's disease was increasingly debilitating and although Lichtenberger tried at first to carry on, by 1964 it was clear to him that retirement was inevitable. His opening address to the convention which met in St. Louis was a moving reaffirmation of some fundamental convictions. The Right Rev. Ned Cole, Bishop Coadjutor of Central New York, read it for him. Lichtenberger began by acknowledging that all did not agree with his convictions about the relevance of the gospel to the great social issues:

"During the past few months I have received many letters criticising our National Council or the House of Bishops, or me, for expressing our opinions . . . in areas which they say are not religious. Here, out of hundreds I might read you is one example . . . 'Instead of you sticking to religion and having our bishops dress up and conduct confirmation services, like the heads of our religion, you want them to get mixed up with minority groups, with issues that have nothing to do with religion.' Surely . . . not many would make such a sharp distinction between religion and life. But I assure you . . . the notion that what goes on in a church building is quite unrelated to what goes on outside is far more general than I would have thought six years ago."

But this presiding bishop was not about to back down, and he called the Convention once again to a vision of its mission:[65]

"When we separate the Christian faith from life, we are cutting ourselves off from God the Father, and Jesus Christ, His Son, and the Holy Spirit . . . [We must be] concerned in every aspect of our lives, in our homes, in business and industry, in the complex social and political issues which confront us."

It was a stirring call to engage the great national issues of the day.

As the convention began its business, it became clear that Arthur Lichtenberger had not finished his message. In his opening address, he had urged Convention to permit the seating of women deputies.[66] Nonetheless, the House of Deputies by a close vote refused to seat them. The next day, Lichtenberger broke precedent by sending an extraordinary rebuke to the Deputies:[67]

"What I have to say now I speak in the utmost charity; but I know I must speak; and I shall try to speak the truth, as I see it, in love.

"When I heard yesterday of the action of the House of Deputies about the women of our Church I was greatly disturbed. It is not my own personal feelings that are involved here, but my deepest conviction.

"Then today, after the Eucharist this morning, and now our commitment to Mutual Responsibility and Interdependence in the Body of Christ, the contrast between what was done yesterday and today is very great.

"Does this mean that what we did this morning, in offering ourselves to God, and after the women presented with grateful hearts their United Thank Offering of prayer and gifts and joyful service, and our declaration of mutual responsibility, — that all this is a travesty? No, it was quite the other way. What we did this morning and what we do now is reality — the other is, I believe, the unwillingness to face the fact that women are members of the Body of Christ, that they are of the laity and members of the Body of Christ."

As far as I know, no previous presiding bishop in the history of this church had ever sent a message of this nature to the House of Deputies.

Lichtenberger was, of coure, not alone in his concern for a greater involvement by the church in the issues of justice and freedom. Prior to the 1964 Convention, an open letter by 140 prominent lay and clerical members of this church called for greater response to the issues of justice and poverty:[68]

"A clear statement by the House of Bishops on the immorality of poverty in a society of plenty can greatly strengthen the actions of clergy and laity in the Church who are working to bring about needed changes."

On October 17, 1964 the House of Bishops assembled in executive session in the nave of Christ Church Cathedral to elect a new presiding bishop. "The Veni Creator Spiritus was said. Silence was observed for a space and the Service to be used before Balloting was concluded." On the sixth ballot the Right Rev. John Elbridge Hines, Bishop of Texas, was elected. Later that day the House of Deputies confirmed the election "by an overwhelming majority."[69]

*   *   *

The election of John Hines was a striking affirmation of the prophetic vision which Arthur Lichtenberger had enunciated. Born in 1910, Hines had graduated from Virginia Theological Seminary, served parishes in Missouri and Georgia, and had been rector of Christ Church, Houston when he was elected Bishop Coadjutor of Texas in 1945. He had succeeded as Bishop of Texas in 1955, and the ten years since 1955 have been described as "crucial years" in the life of that diocese. From the beginning Hines urged the diocese to face the tense issues of segregation and racism. In his first address to the Diocese of Texas as bishop in 1956 he told the delegates, "The Church can no longer move uncertainly in the unclear atmosphere created by this dramatic aspect of a social and cultural revolution, but must now speak and act according to the obligations of Christian statesmanship." During the next ten years Bishop Hines acted courageously and often controversially in a variety of social issues. In 1963, for example, St. Stephen's School became the first desegregated coeducational boarding school in the south. At the same time, opposition began to be expressed in terms of falling income, and two capital funds drives failed. The chairman of the Christian Social Relations department of the diocese, William Gardner Winters, recalled the events of those days in words that were prophetic of Hines' term as presiding bishop:

"The position of John E. Hines on the race issue was crystal clear. The apostles of segregation knew that the diocesan had control of the institutions and missions of the diocese through the power of appointment. They also knew that the mission clergy were a source of strength for the diocesan bishop and that the institutions of the diocese would eventually have to conform to the will of the bishop. However, without additional capital funds there would be fewer opportunities to appoint mission clergy and the debt ridden institutions would not be free to implement the controversial policies of Bishop Hines. Accordingly, many disgruntled laymen either reduced the amount of their contributions or refused to contribute to the capital funds drives in an attempt to squelch this liberal genie who was their bishop."

Charles Henery, in his study of the episcopate of John Hines, reached this conclusion:[70]

"The *issue of conflict* during Bishop Hines' episcopate in Texas largely centered on *racial* and *fiscal* policies. The year 1947 may be considered the beginning evolution of a diocesan consciousness on the race issue; it was in this year that Bishop Hines warned the Council of the "keg of dynamite" in their midst. The Supreme Court ruling of 1954 outlawing segregation in public schools — together with removal of the General Convention scheduled in Houston in 1955 — served to heighten the problem of the black-white situation in the life of the Texas diocese. Bishop Hines moved steadily to integrate diocesan camps, hospitals, schools and other institutions. He understood the emotional difficulties surrounding the racial issue, and he consistently acted within the authorized actions of the diocesan Council."

Bishop Hines had been unswerving in his commitment to an involved and responsive church, and he would bring those commitments with him to the Executive Council. Asked by a reporter for his response shortly after his election as presiding bishop, Hines replied that he was surprised, overwhelmed, and not sure what to say. He went on at once, however, to ". . . pinpoint the chief issues facing the Church: the relationship between the races, the industrial revolution, and the church's relevance to the social order in these days of great change."[71]

The General Convention of 1964 passed one other significant resolution which, in part, dealt with the office of Presiding Bishop. The Committee on Social and International Affairs reported to the House of Bishops that they had prepared a statement on "Levels of Authority within the Church." The resolution was adopted by the bishops and a few days later by the deputies. It is a striking resolution and the most careful official effort to distinguish different levels of authority which this church has made. Recognizing the rights of all Christians to bear witness to the gospel "in every phase of human life and activity," the report went on to declare that Christians must speak "out of the context of their own levels of authority and responsibility." The resolution identified four such levels: the General Convention (itself subject to the Holy Scriptures and the creeds); the House of Bishops; the Presiding Bishop and the Executive Council;

and the officers and staff of the Executive Council. The occasion for the report was probably the so-called "Stringfellow incident,"[72] when there was some confusion about the official or unofficial character of a statement issued by Mr. William Stringfellow. But the significance of the joint resolution goes far beyond that incident. The authority of the presiding bishop and council were explicitly placed within a hierarchy of authorities, subordinate to the authority of General Convention and the House of Bishops but acknowledged as an official voice of this church with far-reaching authority.[73]

"3. In the interim of General Convention, the Presiding Bishop and the Executive Council are the responsible representatives of the Church, granted authority to implement the statements and actions of General Convention and of the House of Bishops. When, in the course of the fast-moving events of life today, it is not possible to await a meeting of General Convention, it is the duty of the Presiding Bishop and the Executive Council to speak God's word to his Church and to his world."

In large part this report simply sets forth clearly the common understanding of the interrelated and ascending orders of authority of presiding bishop and Executive Council, House of Bishops, and General Convention. The one new note was to authorize a responsibility which the Convention of 1937 had been unwilling to approve. It was now the duty of the presiding bishop and Executive Council "to speak God's word to his Church and to his world."

In 1963 Bishop Lichtenberger had appointed a Committee on Mutual Responsibility to respond to the summons issued by the Primates and Metropolitans of the Anglican Communion that year. They presented their report in 1964 recognizing in that summons "a call to a sweeping renewal and re-organization of the life and work of the Church." Convention enthusiastically responded to the report, authorized a voluntary giving program of six million dollars for the next three years for "projects of responsible co-operative partnership with other Churches of the Anglican Communion" and established "an agency of the General Convention, under the direction of the Presiding Bishop, to be named The Mutual Responsibility Commission" charged with stimulating and supporting this effort.[74]

That Commission was duly appointed by Bishop Hines. The Right Rev. Thomas H. Wright, Bishop of East Carolina, was chairman; Mr. Walker Taylor, Jr. was executive officer; twenty-two other members and thirteen consultants made up the commission. That commission or its executive committee met many times during 1966 and presented an extensive and thorough report to the General Convention of 1967. For our purposes, one of the most important decisions of the commission was made on March 12, 1966 when the commission turned its attention to the structure of the Church as a basic question for any significant renewal. On May 18th that decision was stated:[75]

"The renewal of the Church in its total mission requires that the structure and strategy of the Church as organization be subject to a fundamental review.

"Specifically, it is important that the relationship among the Office of the Presiding Bishop, the General Convention, and the Executive Council be examined in respect of their effectiveness in fulfilling common responsibilities for decision-making, administration and communications."

The extensive minutes of that commission make clear the careful studies which they undertook. Consultants were engaged and many lines of investigation were explored. Conferences were held with former presiding bishops. The dangers of concentrating on structure were recognized early in their meetings: "If this appears to the

Deputies to be merely another management study, the Commission will be dead." The strengths and weaknesses of the office of Presiding Bishop were fully studied and considered; that discussion lies behind the numerous recommendations made by the Commission. They had little sympathy with earlier ideas of a special see for the presiding bishop. In the 1960s it was seen as "artificial, sentimental and archaic." But they were concerned about making the presiding bishop more responsible for the overall program of the church and more effectively involved in all the national activities of the church. Thus it was important that he "have the duty" to appear at sessions of the House of Deputies, that he be *ex officio* a member of all joint committees and commissions, that he be seen as "Chief Pastor," and that he travel and visit widely in the church.[76]

The Commission finally made nine proposals for the office of Presiding Bishop and embodied these in a proposed series of canonical and constitutional changes.

1. That the presiding bishop can be canonically identified as "Chief Pastor."

2. That his pastoral responsibilities be met by requiring him to visit every jurisdiction.

3. That he be charged with "giving leadership" in initiation and development of policy and strategy in this church.

4. That he, and the president of the House of Deputies, be *ex officio* members of all joint commissions and committees.

5. That he be allowed such "personal assistants" as may be necessary.

6. That he be given an "Advisory Council."

7. That his term of office be twelve years.

8. That he be elected directly by the entire General Convention (rather than election by the House of Bishops with confirmation by the House of Deputies).

9. That his successor be elected three years prior to his

retirement so that careful orientation of the new presiding bishop would be possible.

Thus the commission defined its proposals. However, its canonical recommendations touched a new note which was not clearly identified in the proposals. The commission recommended that Canon 2, Section 4(a), (2) be worded: The Presiding Bishop shall "speak God's word to his Church and to the world as the representative of this Church and its episcopate in its corporate capacity."[77] That which the Convention of 1937 had failed to pass, and which the Convention of 1964 had accepted by resolution as a responsibility of the presiding bishop and Council was now proposed as a canonical duty of the presiding bishop alone.

The report of the Mutual Responsibility Commission was easily the most thorough and considered set of recommendations about the office of Presiding Bishop ever to be presented to a General Convention. Some fifteen years later it is easier to see the weaknesses in the report. There was little sense in the commission's deliberations of the history of the office or of the many issues which had been raised about that office in the past. The commission did recognize that too much was expected of a presiding bishop, but the report of the commission did not help much. In effect three distinct images of the office, all of which have shorter or longer precedents in this church, were combined. The office was to be a combination of chief executive officer, chief pastor, and prophetic witness. Although the recommendations of the commission were not accepted by Convention without amendment, all three images are still clearly articulated in the present canons.

Shortly after John Hines took office as presiding bishop, he sent a letter to every bishop in this church asking for "suggestions which could make the office of Presiding Bishop more effective in the life of the church." He received replies from many bishops. All showed a sense of appreciation at the inquiry, and many had clearly given much thought and reflection to their answer. One impression stands out very clearly from those answers, namely the varied and often contradictory hopes and expectations which different bishops had for John Hines. Many wanted him to be a pastor and spiritual leader. Others hoped he would be a moral force or a spokesman for the national church on great issues. Others saw him as "quarterback" at the Episcopal Church Center directing the work of that body effectively and efficiently. Still others hoped he would be flexible enough to respond to the varied and pluralistic nature of this church. All of the great images which have been applied to the office were touched upon by those bishops, but there was no clear consensus and no common understanding of the position.[78]

The pivotal year for this church and for the episcopate of John Hines was 1967. In August of that year, in the wake of the urban riots, Bishop Hines took two walking tours in Bedford-Stuyvesant, Brooklyn, and in Detroit. The tours were a conversion experience for him. He was determined that the church must act, and when the General Convention met in Seattle in 1967, he called the church to an "urban crisis program." In a magnificent opening sermon the presiding bishop set forth his hopes and goals. After describing the "crisis in American cities" he issued this call:[79]

"As at least the beginning of this Church's response to the deep human need dramatized by the conflict in the cities I am recommending the development of a program to be extended over the next triennium , by which this Church can take its place, humbly and boldly, alongside of, and in support of, the dispossessed and oppressed peoples of this country for the healing of our national life. Among its aims will be the bringing of peoples in ghettos into areas of decision making by which their destiny is influenced.

It will encourage the use of political and economic power to support justice and self-determination for all men. It will make available skilled personnel assistance, and request the appropriation of substantial sums of money to community organizations involved in the betterment of depressed urban areas, and under the control of those who are largely both black and poor, that their power for self-determination may be increased and their dignity restored.

"I am requesting the funding of such a program in the amount of approximately $3 million annually, and funds to be secured from various sources, principally from the General Church program."

The Convention responded with enthusiasm: "The focus of our outward response is to be on enabling the poor, especialy the ghetto-poor, to gain an effective voice and visible presence in the decisions which affect their own lifes." Thus began a program which was soon called by the Executive Council the "General Convention Special Program," or GCSP. Never before in the history of this church has a presiding bishop been able to gather up the hopes and fears, the ideals and aspirations of many, many deputies, and to channel those into a dramatic new program involving millions of dollars. One observer wrote that

"The Seattle General Convention, in response to the Presiding Bishop . . ., committed itself to what has been called the most radical and ambitious national program carried out by a white American church in the field of race relations."

And John Hines himself declared the Seattle General Convention to be "the most constructive he's ever attended."[80]

The Seattle convention also received the Report of the Mutual Responsibility Commission. Although a few recommendations were not approved, most of the report was adopted by the 1967 Convention and read into

116

Canon 2, "Of the Presiding Bishop."

After all the debate about the office, it is something of a surprise to realize that prior to 1967 the canons said remarkably little about the nature of the office. Details of election, terms of office and traditional duties were covered. But nowhere in Canon 2 was there any clear conception of the office. A major effort to change that was made in 1967.

There was much interest in the report of the Mutual Responsibility Commission. *The Witness* declared that the report was "of such importance to all Episcopalians that we are printing all of it," and *The Living Church* supported the proposals with enthusiasm. The presiding bishop

> ". . . is expected to lead the Church, but he is given extraordinarily little actual power of command. Bishop Butterfield of Vermont is right in saying, 'There's been a good deal of guilt feeling about what we've been doing to the Presiding Bishop. We expect him to be the big man out front, but we haven't given him the authority, time or manpower to do the job.' . . . We are strongly inclined to agree with those who urge a decided strengthening of this office."[81]

At Seattle the Convention adopted much of the substance of the commission's report. Convention was unwilling to appoint a canonical Council of Advice to the Presiding Bishop, and the House of Bishops were unwilling to give up their right to elect that person. Nor did Convention approve the election of a successor three years before his term began. But the changes which were introduced into Canon 2 were considerable. The presiding bishop was defined as the "chief pastor." He was responsible for "initiating and developing the policy and strategy of the Church." He was to "speak God's words to the Church and to the world, as the representative of this Church." He was given greater authority over the General

Convention and was charged to "visit every Diocese of this Church." He was to report annually to the church and could "from time to time, issue Pastoral Letters in his own person." He could appoint officers who were "responsible to him, to whom he may delegate so much of his authority as to him shall seem appropriate." And he was now a member *ex officio* of all joint committees and commissions with the right to send a personal representative who had no vote.[82] For the first time in the canonical history of this church, a clear statement of responsibilities and duties for the presiding bishop was made. And, as in the report of the Mutual Reponsibility Commission, three clear images are enshrined in the canon: chief pastor, chief executive officer, prophetic leader.

*　　　*　　　*

An account of the development of GCSP, of its many achievements and of the growing opposition to its development, is too vast a topic to consider here. A special General Convention was held at Notre Dame, Indiana in the summer of 1969. Already it was clear that opposition to GCSP might be affecting the national income of the church. Perhaps more important was the sense of difficult and unavoidable issues which could not but be divisive. An article in *The Episcopalian,* reporting on the Notre Dame Convention, expressed the mood:[83]

"The anxieties had been gathering since Seattle. Many dioceses protested the legality of the format for Special Convention II; the so-called Black Manifesto had opened new wounds in a Church not yet able to heal the old ones. Other voices of people within the Church — black, young, female, Indian, Latin — struggled for expression. All these frustrations were dropped in the Church's lap at Notre Dame."

The 1969 Convention had little time to consider the

role of presiding bishop, but one report and one extraordinary comment did emerge. The Joint Commission on Structure (who had felt some overlapping of their responsibilities with the work of the Mutual Responsibility Commission in 1966-1967) reported in 1969 that the changes made two years earlier in Seattle had "made little difference" in the office of Presiding Bishop and they proposed that major responsibility for national administration be given to a "presidency" composed of the presiding bishop, the president of the House of Deputies, and a new chairman of the Executive Council (now to be called the General Board). Their recommendations were not adopted, but the Commission also read into the record a striking letter from the Very Rev. John Coburn, then Dean of the Episcopal Theological School. In effect, Coburn cautioned against too great centralization of authority in the office of Presiding Bishop:

"In his office are joined the legislative authority of the House of Bishops and the administrative authority of the Executive Council . . . From the point-of-view of the traditional balance-of-power concept, it raises questions. When legislative and executive functions are merged, questions of adequate representation of the constituency always arise sooner or later . . . It is almost as though the president of a university were also president of the Board of Trustees."

And turning to the conflicts then developing, Coburn concluded:[84]

"It is probably not recognized throughout the Church that such identification of administration and policy functions in office is the fact. This matter of "process" may be more the cause of some of the unrest in the Church around the GCSP than the Program itself — though the problem may not be recognized."

The next four years, from 1969 to 1973, saw both the

effective work of the GCSP and growing opposition to that program. Declining national budgets required drastic action. The General Convention of 1970 imposed considerable restriction on the GCSP, and in December of that year the staff of the national headquarters was reduced from 204 to 110. The Joint Commission on Structure had retained a Chicago-based management firm, Booz-Allen & Hamilton, Inc., to evaluate the work of the church. Their report declared that the role of the presiding bishop was still vaguely defined and that he was assigned too many responsibilities:[85]

> "The skills that appear to be required to fulfill the important symbolic, prophetic, pastoral, and leadership responsibilities are quite distinct from the administrative skills required of a chief executive . . . The concept of the Presiding Bishop has not been fully reconciled with the concept of autonomy of the bishops in the dioceses."

And the commission itself reported to Convention that "at no time since he became a full-time elected person" has the church in General Convention, or anywhere else, really thought through the nature of the office and the effect of all the responsibilities placed upon the office.[86]

Shortly after the Houston Convention of 1970, Bishop Hines appointed a "Consultant Group" to make recommendations to him about a definition of the office. They reported on February 2, 1972:[87]

> "We assumed . . . we would arrive at a clearer definition of the job of the Presiding Bishop, and might even be able to write a sort of job description . . . We are now convinced that this would be very unwise. One of the real strengths of the office — and of the church — is to elect a first-rate man and then establish a situation in which he is free to exercise his own talents — and graces — be they pastoral, prophetic, administrative, or other. The varieties of talents brought by a succession of Presiding Bishops

is essential to the vitality of the church."

On May 1, 1972 John Hines announced his decision to retire as presiding bishop: "The Church will be better served by the election in 1973 of a younger and more vigorous person." I have referred earlier to the important and balanced research study of John Hines which was done by Charles Henery, a doctoral student at General Theological Seminary. Fr. Henery concluded with this estimate of Bishop Hines:[88]

"For some in the Church John Hines was and is a great social prophet who recognized the desperate needs of his own time. For others he was 'a prisoner of the militant rhetoric' of the age who could not truly listen to the pastoral problems of the Church he served. His critics faulted him for not being able to evaluate objectively the criticism against the people he chose for his administrative staff or the techniques and policies of his administration. Whether people agreed or disagreed with him, however, there is no evidence that anyone ever questioned John Hines' integrity or courage.

"John Hines was able to summon a Church to battle, but as the war carried on, it became increasingly difficult to maintain morale or summon forth new energy. He could sound the trumpet because he was singularly gifted with the power of persuasion. He could not, however, preserve the vision of the rightness of the struggle in the eyes of many. Yet, no one could escape the truth of what he said. Once John Hines set his hand to the plow, there was no turning back for him — and this was a sign of his faithfulness and his discipleship."

The image of the presiding bishop as a prophetic voice, speaking God's word to the church, was a fairly recent one. It was first clearly articulated in 1937 and first embodied in any official action in 1964. More than any other, however, that understanding of the office seems to have been the one embraced by John Hines. Far more than any other presiding bishop in our history, Hines sought to engage this church directly in great social issues of race, poverty, and justice. His ability to do so in the dramatic moments of the convention at Seattle was a remarkable testimony both to his witness and to the power of the office of Presiding Bishop. And his inability to persuade the church to continue in that kind of advocacy role with that kind of involvement was an equally remarkable testimony to the limits which are inevitable in the office.

The House of Bishops met in 1972 after Hines had announced his intention to retire. Inevitably, the House spent some time considering once again the nature of the office. That discussion made it clear that there was still no satisfactory understanding.

"We want the Presiding Bishop to be prophet, pastoral leader, symbol of unity, flexible chief liturgist . . . Many urged very strongly a great deal of delegation, especially in the administrative area. Some urged consideration of separating the administrative function from the office, so the Presiding Bishop could be "Chairman of the Board" rather than President. Members suggested consideration of a different title to clarify the Church's expectations of the office."[89]

At the General Convention in Louisville, Kentucky in 1973, the Right Rev. John Maury Allin, Bishop of Mississippi, was elected the twenty-third presiding bishop. It would seem neither appropriate nor possible to offer any significant historical comments on the present presiding bishop. The only significant canonical change took place in 1976 when the members of the national staff were made accountable directly and clearly to the presiding bishop. In many ways this action streamlined and clarified that administrative issue.

But many of the issues about the office as it developed

in the late nineteenth and early twentieth centuries are still unsettled. It remains, therefore, to identify those issues and questions.

Notes

[1] The canon implied that requirement, and a report in 1925 interpreted the canon that way. General Convention, *Journal,* 1925, p. 27.

[2] White, *Constitution and Canons, Annotated,* p. 401.

[3] *The Living Church,* April 28, 1923: 903.

[4] The full report is in Appendix One.

[5] General Convention, *Journal,* 1925, pp. 27-9.

[6] *The Living Church,* October 19, 1929: 825.

[7] Ibid., November 2, 1929: 914.

[8] *Spirit of Missions,* January, 1930: 6.

[9] *The Living Church,* November 30, 1929: 152.

[10] Episcopal Church Archives, RC 22-2.

[11] See, for example, Convention of Rhode Island, *Journal,* 1931, pp. 48-64.

[12] General Convention, *Journal,* 1934, p. 325; Convention of Rhode Island, *Journal,* 1935, p. 26.

[13] General Convention, *Journal,* 1934, pp. 362-3.

[14] *The Churchman,* October 20, 1934.

[15] *The Living Church,* October 23, 1937: 514.

[16] General Convention, *Journal,* 1934, pp. 198-9.

[17] *The Living Church,* October 16, 1937: 491.

[18] See Appendix Two.

[19] General Convention, *Journal,* 1937, pp. 486-9.

[20] Ibid., pp. 178-80.

[21] Ibid., p. 39.

[22] General Convention, *Journal,* 1937, pp. 352-3; *The Churchman,* October 20, 1937.

[23] General Convention, *Journal,* 1937, pp. 180-1.

[24] Ibid., pp. 350-1 (Emphasis added).

[25] *The Living Church,* October 23, 1937: 501.

[26] Howard Chandler Robbins, *General Convention in 1937,* p. 11.

[27] Convention of Virginia, *Journal,* 1938, p. 30.

[28] Charles W. Sherrin, "Profile of a Presiding Bishop," pp. 84, 85.

[29] General Convention, *Journal,* 1940, pp. 27-8.

[30] Sherrin, p. 86.

[31] General Convention, *Journal,* 1940, p. 290.

[32] Ibid., pp. 515-6.

[33] Charles Gilbert, 1981 Johnson Lectures (unpublished), p. 14.

[34] General Convention, *Journal,* 1940, pp. 252-3.

[35] Convention of Virginia, *Journal,* 1943, pp. 32-3.

[36] *The Living Church,* October 10, 1943: 11-20.

[37] For a reprint of "A Just and Durable Peace" see H. Shelton Smith, et al., *American Christianity: An Historical Interpretation with Representative Documents,* 2:522-6.

[38] General Convention, *Journal,* 1943, p. 571.

[39] Ibid., p. 448.

[40] Ibid., p. 55.
[41] Ibid., p. 281.
[42] Ibid., p. 135.
[43] Convention of Virginia, *Journal*, 1944, p. 40.
[44] General Convention, *Journal*, 1946, pp. 454-6.
[45] Ibid., p. 275.
[46] Ibid., pp. 277, 279.
[47] *The Living Church*, September 22, 1946: 29.
[48] General Convention, *Journal*, 1946, pp. 343-7, 147.
[49] Henry Knox Sherrill, *Among Friends*, pp. 105-6.
[50] See above, pp. 85.; Conference with Goldwaite Sherrill, August 21, 1981; Sherrill, *Among Friends*, p. 217.
[51] Episcopal Church Archives, RC 26-11-6.
[52] Sherill, *Among Friends*, p. 327.
[53] *The Living Church*, July 20, 1958: 3.
[54] Ibid., October 12, 1958: 18.
[55] General Convention, *Journal*, 1958, p. 298. A proposal from Maine to reactivate the Committee on a See for the Presiding Bishop failed for the same reason. Ibid., p. 300.
[56] *The Living Church*, October 12, 1958: 16-17.
[57] Episcopal Church Archives, RG43, Box 1, p. 5.
[58] *The Living Church*, September 24, 1961: 11-13, 18.
[59] Ibid., October 8, 1961: 30; September 24, 1961: 12.
[60] Ibid.: 25.
[61] Ibid.: 30.
[62] Episcopal Church Archives, RG43, Box 1.
[63] Arthur Lichtenberger, *The Day is at Hand*, p. 113.
[64] See above, p. 85.
[65] *The Living Church*, October 25, 1964: 10-12, 22.
[66] Lichtenberger had felt strongly about that point for many years. I recall his making a strong point of the injustice of denying women a right to representation in the House of Deputies when he was a professor at General Theological Seminary.
[67] General Convention, *Journal*, 1964, pp. 127-8.
[68] *The Living Church*, October 4, 1964: 19.
[69] General Convention, *Journal*, 1964, pp. 350-1.
[70] Charles Henery, Research project on John Elbridge Hines, Bishop of Texas, 1955-1965.
[71] *The Living Church*, October 25, 1964: 5.
[72] It is so described in the index of the General Convention, *Journal*, 1964, p. 1074.
[73] Ibid., pp. 312-4.
[74] Ibid., pp. 722-30, 324-30.
[75] Report of the Mutual Responsibility Commission to the Sixty-Second General Convention, p. 3.
[76] Episcopal Church Archives, RG-28-8.
[77] Report of the Mutual Responsibility Commission to the Sixty-Second General Convention, pp. 5-6, 39. — COVER
[78] Episcopal Church Archives, RG113-2-1.

79 See Henery, 1967.
80 Ibid.
81 *The Witness,* April 27, 1967; *The Living Church,* May 14, 1967.
82 General Convention, *Journal,* 1967, p. 321.
83 *The Episcopalian,* October, 1969:
84 General Convention, *Journal,* 1969, pp. 46, 377-8.
85 Henery, 1971.
86 General Convention, *Journal,* 1970, p. 722.
87 Ibid., 1973, p. 1094.

4: The Nature of the Office

In 1970 the Joint Commission on Structure reported to General Convention that there was still much to think through about "the nature of the office and the effect of all the responsibilities placed upon" the presiding bishop.[1] It seems clear that the need is still a very current one.

Virtually all long-lived human communities change dramatically over the course of generations. A common western pattern is to retain the names of significant offices and institutions while altering fundamentally the meaning of the office and the responsibilities of officers. The development of the British Constitution is an obvious example, and students of American history have found a similar story in our shorter history. The office of presiding bishop is a fine example of this process. In 1789 that office seems to have been little more than an afterthought, a necessary convenience for the functioning of a tiny House of Bishops. As this church developed its first understanding of its identity as a stable, conservative, rock-like body faithful to the apostolic church, a presiding bishop who was liturgically and sometimes literally the senior bishop was appropriate and suitable. He was in every way a venerable patriarch. Of course, such a person could be far more than a figurehead; the short but enormously effective term of John Henry Hopkins demonstrated the power that could be exercised in moments of crisis. But the symbolic character predominated. It was expressed primarily not in administrative or prophetic ways, but at consecrations of bishops and in pastoral issues. Only occasionally have I referred to the many pastoral situations — often painful ones — which called for ministry from the presiding bishop. There is no need here to resurrect old and forgotten hurts. But the correspondence of every presiding bishop that I could examine made it clear that a considerable part of his time and energy went into such a ministry. When the canon of 1967 described the presiding bishop as "chief pastor," it pointed to an activity which — especially as far as the other bishops of this church were concerned — had often been his careful and caring vocation.

By the late nineteenth century it was clear that old understandings of this church and the presiding bishop were increasingly being questioned. A national church, called to national leadership, needed a different kind of presiding bishop. Only slowly was it possible to redefine the office. The Convention of 1919 did so after many earlier attempts to provide for an elected presiding bishop had failed. For that Convention, the image of a chief executive officer leading and directing the mission of the church was uppermost. But almost immediately that image began to be questioned and expanded. A chief pastor and a chief executive officer are not the same thing, and by 1925 (when the first presiding bishop was actually elected) both images were widely circulating in this church. In the late 1950s still a third note entered — namely a prophetic role as one who is to speak God's word to the church and world. That was clearly emerging in the episcopate of Arthur Lichtenberger and was the dominant theme of the term of John Hines.

Present confusion about the office of presiding bishop is, I think, only part of a larger transition. For many reasons, the national church vision which was powerful in this church for almost a century, has itself come under attack — or is increasingly seen to be irrelevant. The subject is too large a one to explore here, but many of the marks of that "second myth" have disappeared or are disappearing, often for very good reasons: A male-dominated church, worship in Elizabethan language and centered for the most part in Morning Prayer and sermon with Anglican chant, a strict and even rigid attitude toward divorce, a pivotal place within the ecumenical movement as the only "bridge" between protestantism and catholicism, an expanding membership with an unusually high strength among the powerful and wealthy —all of these were marks of the Episcopal Church during the past century. Recently Stephen Sykes began his study of *The Integrity of Anglicanism* with a chapter entitled, "The Crisis of Comprehensiveness." And although William Coats' recent articles, "The Agony of the Episcopal Church" seem somewhat overstated to me, they point to the same kind of crisis of identity.

If this analysis is even partly true, it is clear that any effort to clarify the role of the presiding bishop will be doubly difficult and uniquely important. Confusion about the role only reflects a larger uncertainty about the church itself.

Early in this study I began to explore a comparison of the presiding bishop with the other chief bishops, archbishops, primates, or metropolitans of the Anglican Communion. It soon became clear that that would be a major project rivaling the scope of this present study. Nor did it seem to offer too much help in considering our problem. There is great variety in the Anglican Communion, and it seems clear that the American church has largely developed its structures to meet its needs here and only rarely been influenced in any fundamental way by developments in other countries or cultures.

At one point, however, that comparison did seem helpful; and it has come up many times for debate in this church. The title "Presiding Bishop" has been the subject of many proposals; and it does stand out as virtually unique in the Anglican Communion. There has even been debate about whether terms are to be in upper case or lower case letters. Referred to in the early nineteenth century as "presiding Bishop" (a descriptive title of the presiding officer of the House of Bishops), it later became "Presiding Bishop." Even in 1967 when the presiding bishop was described in Canon Two as "chief pastor", the Deputies insisted that the title be put in lower case letters![2] So it goes.

The title of "Presiding Bishop" does stand out as distinctive when one looks at the chief bishops of other members of the Anglican Communion. The latest *Episcopal Church Annual* lists them this way:

Archbishop of Sydney, Metropolitan of the Province of New South Wales, Primate of Church of England in Australia

Primate, Igreja Episcopal do Brasil

Archbishop of Rangoon and Metropolitan of the Province of Burma

Archbishop of Burundi, Rwanda, and Zaire

Primate of the Anglican Church of Canada

Archbishop of Central Africa and Bishop of Botswana

President of (Casa) Consejo Anglicano Sud Americano

Archbishop of Canterbury, Primate of All England and Metropolitan

Archbishop of the Indian Ocean and Bishop of Mauritius

Archbishop of Armagh, Primate of All Ireland and Metropolitan

Presiding Bishop and Bishop of Kobe (Japan)[3]

President of the Central Synod and Bishop of Iran

Archbishop of the Province of Kenya and Bishop of Nairobi

Archbishop of the Province of Melanesia and Bishop of the Diocese of Central Melanesia

Archbishop of New Zealand

Archbishop of Nigeria and Bishop of Ibadan

Primus of the Scottish Episcopal Church

Archbishop of Capetown and Metropolitan of the Church of the Province of Southern Africa

Archbishop of Sudan and Bishop of Juba

Archbishop of Tanzania

Archbishop of Uganda

Archbishop of Wales and Bishop of Bangor

Archbishop of West Africa

Bishop of the Windward Islands and Archbishop of the West Indies

In 1967 the Mutual Responsibility Commission considered and rejected a recommendation that the title "Archbishop" be used. The proposal can be dismissed as romantic and sentimental. But it has come up many times in this church; recently *The Living Church* proposed that change in a lead editorial.[4] In 1895 Dr. Green of New York told the General Convention, "There is great power in nomenclature . . . give me the right to select the historic name for a system or institution, and anyone who chooses may have the right to formulate its laws."[5] An increasing number of studies have confirmed Dr. Green's judgment. Cultural anthropologists, including those who are studying American society, emphasize the enormous power and significance of symbols and symbolic actions in providing meaning and direction for any human society. Symbolically, the term "presiding bishop" identifies that person as one who takes charge of a meeting. It accurately described the earliest duties of the presiding bishop. I have wondered many times in the course of preparing this study whether much of the current confusion about the role of presiding bishop is not in part due to the lack of a significant symbolic title which would adequately convey, both intellectually and affectively, the ministry of that unique person.

For most of this church's history, the presiding bishop has also been responsible for a particular diocese. That, of course, is the virtually universal pattern in the rest of the Anglican Communion. This church, however, has never been able successfully to combine the post of an elected presiding bishop who had major responsibilities at the national headquarters with the role of diocesan bishop. But it was something of a surprise to me to learn that Henry Knox Sherrill was the first presiding bishop in this church who was required to resign his diocesan jurisdiction upon election. There seems little interest today in trying to look at that problem now, but it has been a significant one for this church on many occasions in the past.

Certainly the greatest issue which stands out from this study is the question of conflicting roles. Chief executive officer, chief pastor, prophetic voice are three major, frequently invoked, and not easily combined images. There have been three different approaches to dealing with these multiple roles.

One has been to write all three roles into our canons and somehow expect the presiding bishop to fulfill all three. That, in fact, seems to have been the solution adopted by earlier General Conventions; and it seems to be enshrined in the report of the Mutual Responsibility Commission as well. A second has been the frequently expressed hope that it would be possible to define the role more closely, to relieve him of administrative responsibility, perhaps to see him as "Chairman of the Board" with an administrative "President" responsible for the business of the national headquarters. However, no effort at a narrower understanding of the office has succeeded in commending itself to this church. Still a third approach was the report of the Consultant Group who recommended to Bishop Hines in 1972 that the office be left deliberately broad and that each presiding bishop be expected to develop that part of the office which was the natural exercise of his own talents and graces.[6] No doubt there are other possible solutions, but these three stand out as the major ways thoughtful Episcopalians of the past have tried to cope with the issue.

The office of presiding bishop has evolved into one of the most important and influential in this church. Not only does he have considerable administrative authority both within the Episcopal Church Center and within the structure of the General Convention, but also presiding bishops have sometimes been able to move this church in a powerful and dramatic way. When Thomas Clark almost inadvertently described himself as "Presiding Bishop of the Church" in 1900, he spoke perhaps more truly than he realized. It is clear that the presiding bishop is "of the Church", although exactly what that means continues to remain somewhat unclear.

Notes

1 See above, p. 127.
2 General Convention, *Journal,* 1967, 322.
3 So the *Episcopal Church Annual* has it. However, The Right Rev. John M. Watanabie, Bishop of Kokkaido, told me recently that the term "Primate" is universal in Japan.
4 *The Living Church,* May 18, 1980, 12.
5 See above, p. 131.
6 See above, p. 132.

Appendix One

Report of the Committee of the House of Bishops to Consider the Question of the Election of the Presiding Bishop:

The Committee appointed to consider the position and function of the Presiding Bishop beg to present the following Report:

The duties of and the requirements concerning the Presiding Bishop are laid down in Sec. 3 of Art. I. of the Constitution and in Canons 17 and 61, with a few other scattered references in the Canons.

1. The Presiding Bishop must be a Bishop having jurisdiction within the United States. If he should resign his jurisdiction he would cease to be Presiding Bishop. Art. I., Sec. 3.

2. His term of office is six years. Nothing is said, one way or the other, about re-election. Canon 17, Sec. 1.

3. He is to preside over meetings of the House of Bishops reclaiming duties which for thirty-five or forty years have been performed by the Chairman of the House. Canon 17, Sec. 2.

4. He is to take Order for the Consecration of Bishops when duly elected. Canon 17, Sec. 2.

5. He is to be the Executive and administrative head of the missionary, educational and social work of the Church, with the aid of the National Council. Canon 61, Sec. 1 [i.], and Sec. 5 [iii].

6. (a) He is to receive an annual report from each missionary Bishop of his proceedings and of the state and condition of the Church within his Missionary District. Canon 19, Sec. 3.

(b) He is to approve of alterations in the Canons of Missionary Districts. Canon 19, Sec. 4.

(c) He is to take charge of any vacant Missionary

District and to appoint a Bishop to act in his place. Canon 14, Sec. 6.

(d) He is to make provision for the Episcopal care of congregations in foreign lands. Canon 57, Sec. 4, 6, 7 and 9.

7. (a) He is to communicate with the heads of Churches in communion with the Episcopal Church as to the establishment of new foreign Missionary Districts. Canon 19, Sec. 2.

(b) and to notify such officials of any sentence of suspension or deposition of a Bishop. Canon 31, Sec. 7 [ii.].

8. In the case of the trial of a Bishop the charges are first presented to the Presiding Bishop, and in the end he had to pronounce sentence in the case of a charge involving teaching contrary to that of this Church. Canon 26, Sec. 1 and 33, Sec. 5 and 6.

9. There is no hint of there being given to the Presiding Bishop, such as seems to be feared by some, any archiepiscopal powers, authorizing any interference in the internal affairs of a diocese.

It will thus be seen that the Presiding Bishop is not only charged with Canonical relations with other Churches and Communions, but that out of these grow necessarily inevitably a great number of responsibilities affecting other than Canon relations. The Presiding Bishop, for example, would appoint delegates to many Conferences and have to represent the Church in the Religious World upon many occasions and in connection with many movements. He is, to borrow the language of the state, the minister of Foreign Affairs.

Within the Church it is clear that outside the Canonical and Constitutional reponsibility which rests upon him in connection with the missionary work there must come to him a great and increasing number of problems involving that work. These come to him as Presiding Bishop and would necessarily come to him whether he were President of the National Council or not.

It was considerations of this character which weighed with the General Convention in the perfecting of the plan whereby the Presiding Bishop was to be made head of the missionary work. Your Committee on further study of the whole matter is satisfied that this original intention of the Church should be followed and the guidance of the work of the Church placed in the same hand as the responsibility for representing the Church in its relations with other religious bodies and in the life of the nation and the world. Only in such way can opportunities for friction be avoided and concentration of purpose be given to the work and position of the Church. Difficulties would surely arise if two active outstanding men were charged each with responsibilities which must, in many cases, overlap. Moreover, as a lesser, but not unimportant consideration, there would be the necessity of providing for two large salaries instead of one which would be contrary to the generally desired effort to economize; and further two dioceses would be largely deprived of their Bishop's oversight.

Your Committee believes that an immense opportunity is opened to the Church to give and to follow a farsighted unifying spiritual leadership. Administrative duties of the more technical and specialized kind may be largely devolved upon others, but thought for the whole Church, responsibility for the realizing of the Church's unity and guidance of its great policies of work should rest in the Presiding Bishop himself.

The Office being of such importance your Committee believes that careful provision should be made for filling the vacancy in the event of the death or disability of the Presiding Bishop. At present the Constitution provides that the Senior Bishop should succeed automatically and hold office until the next meeting of the General Convention. The responsibility for so large an office might thus fall for three years upon a Bishop who, on account of age or infirmity, would be unable to carry it. It would be desirable, the Committee believes, to provide that the succession should come to the Chairman of the House of Bishops, who would thus hold in effect a kind of Vice-President position. He should, if succeeding to the Presiding Bishopric, hold office until the next General Convention and the Presiding Bishop then elected should be elected for a full term of six years. The Committee offers below resolutions for amendments to the Constitution and Canons covering this matter.

The Committee recommends that the salary of the Presiding Bishop be fixed at $15,000, with an allowance of $5,000 for house rent and expenses, and that the provision for this amount be included in the Budget of the National Council.

In conclusion the Committee again emphasizes the importance of the opportunity which is now offered the Church. However great the demand may be for administrative and executive capacity in the office its supreme opportunity is spiritual. To interpret the Church's growing consciousness of her unity and her mission to the world, to interpret it to both the Church and the world, to lead and inspire, to carry confidence and faith and develop devotion and loyalty, your Committee believes that such is the chief responsibility which will rest upon the Presiding Bishop. The responsibility which, therefore, rests upon this house is proportionately great.

[General Convention, *Journal,* 1925, pp. 27-9.]

Appendix Two

Joint Committee on Status and Work of the Presiding Bishop, to Study all Questions Relating to That Subject and Report to the Convention of 1937:

In its report to the General Convention of 1934, the Committee contented itself with a very simple setting-forth of certain objectives which, it was felt, should be before Convention and the Church at Large, in connection with any consideration of the Status and Work of the Presiding Bishop.

The only one of these objectives which was really discussed, and in regard to which any action was taken by that Convention, was the necessity of giving the Presiding Bishop relief from the details of administrative duty in connection with his presidency of the National Council.

The original recommendation of this Committee in regard to this matter was not adopted by the Convention, but a substitute, originating elsewhere, was passed. In addition, a committee was set up on the Evaluation of the National Council. Further, the National Council appointed a committee from its own membership to consider the reorganization of its administration.

It is increasingly evident that the plan embodied in present Canon 60 is not working well. We are therefore recommending the substitution of the language of Canon 59, Sec. I. (i) of the Canons of 1931 for the language of the present Canon 60 Sec. I. (i) and that the whole of Canon 60 be revised accordingly. In this recommendation the Committee on Evaluation of the National Council agrees with us.

The next objective discussed was the permanency of the office of Presiding Bishop. This would mean his election for life, or, preferably, until a determined age of retirement, instead of his election as at present for a term of six years.

This was recommended, not alone for the sake of the dignity of the office, but to assure the Church of continuity of service. The Committee feels that the Church could be thus assured of a consistency in attitude and opinion over a period of years.

In order to obtain this objective, it would not be necessary to amend the Constitution, but only to amend Canon 17, Section 11, substituting the words, "until the first day of January, succeeding that General Convention which follows his attainment of the age of seventy years" for the present wording. A resolution recommending such an amendment, for reference to the Committee on Canons, is attached to, and forms a part of this report.

The next objective was the relief of the Presiding Bishop from the details of diocesan administrative duty.

Although the wording of the Constitution would permit the election to this office of any Bishop of this Church, ordinarily and especially in view of the Presiding Bishop's relationships with other National Churches, the choice would fall upon the Bishop of a diocese or missionary district. Our experience thus far has compelled us to face the fact that we have no right to ask any man to carry this double burden.

Two ways are open to us. One method would be to require the diocese from which the Presiding Bishop is chosen, to elect at once a Bishop Coadjutor to whom the Presiding Bishop-elect should be required to delegate a jurisdiction which would relieve him of all but nominal duties.

The other method would be the creation of a See for the Presiding Bishop. This could be accomplished either by entering into a concordat with some existing diocese, whereby the right of that diocese to choose its own bishop might be yielded to General Convention; or, by the ceding to General Convention by some existing diocese of a small portion of its territory, which could be erected as a separate diocese over which the Presiding Bishop would have jurisdiction.

However, it does not seem necessary to discuss this question of a See for the Presiding Bishop except in outline in this report. Until some diocese has, through its Bishop and Convention, plainly stated its willingness to enter into such a concordat, or make such a cession of territory, it is hardly competent for this Committee to discuss details of such a plan.

It might not be beyond the Committee's province, however, to say that of all the suggestions that have been made regarding such a See for the Presiding Bishop, that which proposes seeking a concordat with the Diocese of Washington seems to be not only the best, but also that which, in the end will carry the most weight, both in this country and in other lands.

In view of the fact that it might, however, take quite a length of time to think through and to perfect the arrangements for such a See for the Presiding Bishop, this Committee stands ready, if the Convention desires it, to recommend such changes in Canon 17 as will give temporary relief for a Presiding Bishop-elect from the burden of diocesan administration.

It will be noted that the Committee has not concerned itself about nor recommended any change in the title of the office. This position has been taken deliberately. There is no fear of Archbishops as such, nor is there any timidity about opposition to the whole plan, arising from possible dislike of such a title. The title Presiding Bishop has been consecrated for us by the men who have held it. It is part of our national Church life and experience. Moreover, the Presiding Bishop, by virtue of the duties which he now performs is Primate and Metropolitan whatever title he holds. It might be worth our while to pass as resolution in General Convention that whenever the title is printed in official documents these words, "Primate and Metropolitan", should follow such a title, but we make no recommendation.

The Committee is aware that there are those who wish clearer definition in the Constitution of the duties and office of the Presiding Bishop. The Committee doubts the advisability of defining too clearly such duties in a Constitution, which deals with principles rather than with details. At the last General Convention an attempt was made to do this, but the result was not satisfactory and did not commend itself to General Convention. Granted an office of this sort, the men chosen for it will themselves create its traditions.

In reply to those who question the advisability of making any changes at all, we would say that this Church needs, increasingly, a visible symbol of its national unity. Provinces may in the future be given additional powers by General Convention. We may seek to develop a more intelligent policy of Church extension by paying more heed to local needs as shown to us by those who really know them. But we shall need all the more a growing sense of our national responsibility for the work as a whole. No committee like the National Council, or any large assemblage like the General Convention — representative in a way as they are — can ever be as truly symbolic as an individual leader. This accords with the facts of human nature and with the central truth of the Christian Religion — the Incarnation of the Son of God.

This is the Committee's reason for recommending such changes as we have. In case the General Convention decides to adopt the plan of a See for the Presiding Bishop, we feel that another Commission should be appointed to consider and report, and that this Committee, which has served for six years, should be discharged.

The Committee met in New York on September 9, 1937, with the Joint Commission to Evaluate the Activities of the National Council. All members of the Committee were present except the Rev. Mr. Barber and Mr. Taylor. The two Commission were unanimous in the support of the decisions arrived at by the two

Commissions. The following resolutions were adopted:

Resolved, (House of Bishops, House of Deputies) concurring, that Canon 17, Section II., be amended by substituting after the word "office", in the third line, and for what follows up to the period in the fifth line, the following: "until the first day of January succeeding the General Convention which follows his attainment of the age of seventy years."

Resolved, (House of Bishops, House of Deputies) concurring, that a new section be added to Canon 17, to be numbered III., and the succeeding sections to be renumbered accordingly:

"When a diocesan bishop is elected Presiding Bishop, it shall be the duty of the diocese of which he is Bishop to elect a Bishop-Coadjutor forthwith. It shall be the duty of the Presiding Bishop to assign to the Bishop-Coadjutor, when elected and consecrated, such jurisdiction as will relieve the Presiding Bishop of all duties in the diocese which will necessitate his presence therein."

Resolved, (House of Bishops, House of Deputies) concurring, that a commission consisting of three Bishops, three Presbyters and three Laymen, be appointed to discuss the matter of a See for the Presiding Bishop, with the authorities of the Diocese of Washington; that this commission be authorized to enter into necessary preliminary negotiations looking toward that end, and requested to report to the next General Convention.

That it be recommended that old Canon 59, Section 1, paragraph 1, be substituted for present Canon 60, Section 1, paragraph 1, to read as follows:

"The Presiding Bishop and the National Council as hereinafter constituted, shall have charge of the unification, development and prosecution of the Missionary, Educational and Social work of the Church, of which work the Presiding Bishop shall be the executive and administrative head."

Note: Canon 13, Section II., provides that when a Bishop of a Diocese "shall have been elected Presiding Bishop of this Church a Bishop Coadjutor may be elected by the aforesaid Diocese," etc.

Frank A. McElwain,
Chairman

[General Convention, *Journal,* 1937, pp. 486-9.]

BIBLIOGRAPHY

Annual Report of the Presiding Bishop and Council (changed to Annual Report of the National Council), 1920-1962.

Barnds, William Joseph. "A Study of the Development of the Office of Presiding Bishop of the American Episcopal Church, 1794-1944," in *Historical Magazine* (December, 1958): 254-86.

Barnes, C. Rankin. "The General Convention of 1919," in *Historical Magazine* (June, 1952): 224-250.

Barnes, C. Rankin. "The Presiding Bishops of the Church," in *Historical Magazine* (June, 1949): 97-147.

Beardsley, William A. "Thomas Church Brownell—Third Bishop of Connecticut," *Historical Magazine* (December, 1937): 350-69.

Carter, Paul A. *The Spiritual Crisis of the Gilded Age* (Urbana, IL: Northern Illinois University Press, 1971).

Chase, Philander. *Reminiscences: An Autobiography,* 2 vol. (Boston: n.p., 1847).

Cheshire, Joseph B. *The Church of the Confederate States* (N.Y.: Longmans, Green and Co., 1912).

Chorley, E. Clowes. *Men and Movements in the American Episcopal Church* (N.Y.: Charles Scribners' Sons, 1950).

Churchman, The.

Clark, Thomas March. *Reminiscences* (N.Y.: n.p., 1895).

Coleman, Leighton. *Our Ecclesiastical Heritage* (Burlington, VT: Free Press, 1894).

Diocesan *Journals.* Many diocesan journals have been consulted and are cited in the Endnotes. The most complete collections are at the General Theological Seminary and in the Episcopal Church Archives, Austin, Texas.

Doane, George Washington. *The Path of the Just* (Burlington, VT: J. L. Powell, 1836).

Donald, James M. "Bishop Hopkins and the Reunification of the Church," in *Historical Magazine* (1978): 73-91.

Emery, Julia Chester. *A Century of Endeavor: 1821-1921* (N.Y.: The Department of Missions, 1921).

Episcopal Recorder, The.

Executive Council Papers. Found in the Episcopal Church Archives, Austin, Texas.

General Convention. *Journal:* 1789-1979. There is a separate journal published for each General Convention. These have been published by various publishers for the Church.

Guilbert, Charles. "Changes in the Structure, Organization and Governance of the Episcopal Church in the Past Sixty Years." An unpublished study delivered as the 1981 Johnson Lectures.

Henery, Charles R. "The Episcopal Church in Post-Revolutionary New England and New York: 1783-1811." An unpublished paper.

Henery, Charles R. "Research Project for The Episcopal Television Network on John Elbridge Hines, Presiding Bishop." An unpublished report, found at General Theological Seminary, 1980.

Hobart, John Henry. *An Apology for Apostolic Order* (N.Y.: Stanford & Swords, 1846).

Hopkins, John Henry, Jr. *The Life of the Late Right Rev. John Henry Hopkins* (N.Y.: n.p., 1873).

Huntington, William Reed. *The Church Idea: An Essay Towards Unity* (N.Y.: Charles Scribners' Sons, 1899).